your career

Y O U R
career

Coach Yourself
to Success

by Jason R. Rich

LEARNINGEXPRESS
NEW YORK

Library of Congress Cataloging-in-Publication Data:

Rich, Jason R.
    Your career : coach yourself to success / Jason R. Rich.
        p. cm.
    Includes index.
    ISBN 1-57685-362-4 (pbk.)
    1. Career development. 2. Vocational guidance. I. Title.

HF5381 .R48 2001
650.14—dc21   00-067428

Printed in the United States of America

9 8 7 6 5 4 3 2

First Edition

For information on LearningExpress,
other LearningExpress products,
or bulk sales, please write to us at:

LearningExpress
900 Broadway
Suite 604
New York, NY 10003

Or visit our website at:
www.learnatest.com

ⓒ ⓞ ⓝ ⓣ ⓔ ⓝ ⓣ ⓢ

Ⓐ Ⓒ Ⓚ Ⓝ Ⓞ Ⓦ Ⓛ Ⓔ Ⓓ Ⓖ Ⓜ Ⓔ Ⓝ Ⓣ Ⓢ

THIS BOOK IS all about achieving goals and dreams and making the most out of the career-related opportunities you encounter. When it comes to my own career, it's the endless support and encouragement I receive on a daily basis from my two closest friends, Mark Giordani and Ellen Bendremer, that allow me to achieve my own goals and dreams. Thus, I dedicate this book to them, as well as to my family.

I'd also like to thank Brigit Dermott and Jennifer Farthing at LearningExpress for inviting me to work on this book project.

Thanks to my friends Andy Lawson, Nic Womble, and Adam Brewster—members of the pop music group B-Factor (www.BFactorMusic.com)—with whom I have the privilege to work as their manager (outside of my writing career). As this book was being written, we've been traveling throughout Europe on tour, which has provided for a wide range of fun, educational, and sometimes challenging experiences.

Finally, thanks to you, the reader. I hope you find this book to be informative and helpful as you embark on a quest to achieve your own personal, professional, and financial goals. If you'd like to share your experiences, ideas, or comments, please visit my website at http://www.jasonrich.com, or e-mail me at jr7777@aol.com.

INTRODUCTION

YOUR CAREER REPRESENTS much more than a current job. It encompasses all the related, and unrelated, jobs you'll hold from your first paycheck to your retirement. A career path might involve working your way up the corporate ladder and staying with a single employer until retirement (which is becoming increasingly rare), or it might include holding a handful of jobs, working for different employers, but in the same profession, occupation, and/or industry. In addition, many career paths now include changing jobs or professions one or more times and using the variety of skills you learn in different occupations to round out your skill set.

People who ultimately achieve success in their careers aren't lucky and they're probably no different from you. These people have discovered how to plan their career path, set and achieve goals, uncover and take advantage of opportunities, become highly skilled at networking, and they aren't afraid to work hard to obtain what they want out of life.

Those who achieve success have also discovered how to learn from their mistakes, overcome whatever obstacles they face, utilize their time properly, delegate responsibilities, and focus their attention on issues that matter to them, their employer, and to achieving their goals.

Your Career: Coach Yourself to Success was written to help you fully utilize the resources you have available right now and help you learn exactly what it takes to properly manage your career and make your career-related goals a reality. This book will help you determine what skills you will need to help you develop and acquire a road map for achieving success. It does not, however, offer instant solutions or get rich quick schemes.

If you want to be successful in your professional life, no matter what occupation you choose to pursue or what industry you ultimately work in, it's going to take a lot of hard work and dedication to achieve your goals. Throughout your career, you'll probably receive guidance and support from superiors, friends, family, and others, but when it comes to actually making career-related decisions and working your way toward success, you'll need to discover how to rely on yourself and ultimately coach *yourself* to success.

In the first few chapters of this book, you're going to be asked many questions that are designed to help you learn all about yourself, your values, and your aspirations. Your answers to these questions will help you set your personal, professional, and financial goals; determine your likes and dislikes; figure out what specifically you're good at and where your strengths lie; and pinpoint areas where you need improvement.

Once you determine what you're really trying to accomplish in your career, this book will help you develop detailed action plans for achieving those goals. Since long-term goals aren't achievable overnight, you will learn how to build a plan made of a series of smaller steps that will lead you to ultimate goal. So no matter how ambitious your goals might be, you will learn how to stay on task and motivated so you can make the most of your career.

Knowing what you want to achieve is critical, and having a plan to get you there is just as important. *Your Career: Coach Yourself to Success* will also help you develop other vital skills that will lead you to success. When you want more out of your career than a paycheck you need to use your time wisely so that you can spend time learning new skills and having a life outside of work. You will learn time management and organizational skills that can help you get ahead. You'll also learn how to find the ideal job, how to market yourself, and how to develop a network.

Even if you graduated at the top of your class in school and you're about to launch your career, there's a lot you still have to learn that can only be acquired from real-world experience. One of the objectives of this book is to help you combine your traditional education with real-world experience to take full advantage of whatever professional opportunities become available to you. These opportunities will seldom be dropped in your lap, however. Part of achieving success is seeking out your own opportunities and learning how and when to take full advantage of them.

As you make decisions and begin to plan out your future, ideally you want to discover a career path or occupation you're truly passionate about and that inspires you. It will be your passion that will ultimately help keep you motivated as you face the many challenges and obstacles that cross your path on the road to success.

Whether you're first starting out or you already have years of professional experience, one of the most important things you can do to help ensure your long-term success, aside from proper planning and goal setting, is to surround yourself with a positive support system. You want to associate with people whom you admire and care about, and who will offer you the love, support, and guidance you'll need as you confront the challenges of your personal and professional life. Nothing can replace the positive impact of having the support of family, close friends, and a mentor or role model as you face difficult decisions and obstacles that are a common part of everyday life.

Having a strong support system is critical, but developing confidence in yourself and your own abilities is just as important. In your heart, you need to understand what you're trying to accomplish and why, and determine what it will take to achieve what's important to you. As you'll learn from this book, there's a lot more to success than simply having a high-paying job and a fancy job title. Everyone's personal values are different, which means that the decisions you ultimately make should help you work toward the outcomes you're looking to achieve.

Without ignoring the guidance offered by those whom you respect and care about, this book will help you become your own personal career coach. It will help you make your own intelligent career and life-related choices and be confident in your ability to make intelligent decisions with outcomes from which you'll benefit.

Everyone's pathway to success is different. There are no definitive answers for what it will take you to achieve your goals. As you'll soon learn, one of the best ways to determine what pathways to take is to study other people who have achieved success doing whatever it is that interests you, and learn what steps they've taken to make their dreams a reality.

Obviously, since you've begun reading this book, you have the motivation and interest in becoming more successful. *Your Career: Coach Yourself to Success* will help you find your passion and use it to achieve your goals and dreams. Never be afraid to dream . . . but remember, dreaming is only the first step. It's what will inspire you with ideas. To make your dreams become a reality, however, you'll need to take action! If you know in your heart you can accomplish a goal or dream, you can devise a plan to make your dream a reality.

CHAPTER 1

getting to know yourself

CONGRATULATIONS! FOR WHAT, you ask? Well, you've already taken the first step toward achieving success and fulfilling your goals. That's right. First, you identified that there is something missing from your life. In your quest for answers, you purchased this book. That's the first step toward success, and you've done it well!

This book is all about setting goals and fulfilling your short-term and long-term career objectives. However, in the process of improving your employment situation, this book will help you to define and achieve personal and financial goals as well.

Millions of people spend their entire professional life being miserable on the job because they've made bad career decisions. Despite the fact that these people are miserable, they're often unwilling or unmotivated to take the initiative and improve their situation. As a result, they literally dread waking up for work each and every morning. Worst of all, their sole purpose for going to work is to earn a paycheck—and that's it.

Being miserable on the job not only impacts your emotional state during the day when you're at work, but it also has the potential to negatively impact your personal life and even your overall mental and physical health. Furthermore, if you're constantly depressed or fed up with your employment situation, for whatever reason, this often leads to stress, which is something that nobody needs in his or her life. Stress also negatively impacts those around you, including your spouse, siblings, roommates, significant other, co-workers, and friends.

Wouldn't it be great if you could wake up every morning excited to go to work because you truly love your job? Wouldn't you like to spend your time doing things you have a passion for and earn a living in the process? Well, what's holding you back? That's one of the questions this book will help you answer. Once you identify what's keeping you from achieving your professional goals and ambitions, you'll discover how to make the necessary changes in your life so that you can set yourself on a path toward success.

Is this going to be an easy process? Nope. Will it happen overnight? Nope. Do you have what it takes to break away from the path you're on and begin fulfilling your dreams? Yes, but it's going to take hard work, dedication, and a true commitment on your part. If you're willing to put in the time and effort and face obstacles and challenges you encounter head-on, without letting them stand in your way, you can, and will, be successful.

Before you can make positive changes in your life, there are several things you'll need to understand. First, you'll need to be totally, 100% honest with yourself about who you are as a person. In this chapter and the next, you're going to be asked many questions in order to help you get to know yourself better. It's critical that you answer these questions and be brutally honest. Don't worry, you won't ever have to share your answers with anyone else; however, it's important that you write everything down.

Once you've developed a thorough understanding of who you are, you'll need to define exactly what it is you hope to accomplish or achieve in your lifetime. This means setting short-term and long-term goals that are realistic and that relate to your professional life, your personal life, and your financial situation.

As you'll soon discover, one of the tricks to setting goals that are ultimately achievable is to be very specific. General goals like "I want to be a millionaire" or "I want to be the CEO of a company" are not specific. Every goal needs to be backed up by a detailed plan for achieving it, and it needs to be narrowly defined—but more on that later.

Throughout this book, you're going to be discovering tricks for achieving success. However, before you can proceed, it's important to define what success means to you. When you ask yourself what success really means to you, what comes to mind?

Does achieving success mean becoming a highly paid executive? Being able to retire at a young age as a multi-millionaire? Does it mean having a career that you truly love? Does achieving success mean getting married, having kids, and then earning a living to support your family? Does it mean buying an expensive house and a sports car? Do you equate being successful working with a charitable organization and having a positive impact on the lives of others?

Everyone has a different definition for what constitutes success for them personally. According to *Merriam Webster's Collegiate Dictionary*, the definitions of success are: "Degree or measure of succeeding; favorable or desired outcome; the attainment of wealth, favor or eminence; one that succeeds."

Take a few minutes and define *success* for yourself in the following areas:

My definition of personal success is: _____

_____

_____

_____

_____

My definition of professional (career-related) success is: _____

_____

_____

_____

_____

My definition of financial success is: _____

_____

_____

_____

_____

My overall definition of success is: _____

_____

_____

_____

_____

Developing a passion for your work is a key ingredient for success. If you look at almost any highly successful person, one of the primary things that sets him or her apart from others is a passion for whatever it is that he or she does. Because that person has a true love of his or her work, he or she is willing to dedicate whatever effort it takes to excel and achieve success.

Before you have a passion for something, you must determine what your goals are and what types of things you truly enjoy. Knowing this information, it's possible to define a career path for yourself that will allow you to pursue things you love and achieve your goals simultaneously.

As you set out to define your long-term career goals, remember that there's a lot more to life than professional success. Those people who are truly happy are those who have created a well-balanced life, consisting of both work and a personal life. Developing a balance between a personal and professional life is important, because all the professional and financial success in the world means little if you don't have family, loved ones, and close friends to share it with.

There will, no doubt, be times when you'll have to make personal sacrifices in favor of your career (and vice versa). Through careful planning, you should be able to identify, in advance, what these sacrifices will be, and then spend time determining if making each sacrifice is worth it in order to move one or more of your goals closer to fruition. As you work toward success you will need to make decisions that impact your life and the lives of people close to you. You should never, however, make these decisions when you're in a hurry, under pressure, or until you have gathered all of the information you need and have considered all of the various ramifications.

Part of becoming successful means doing research and gathering information, so every decision you make is an educated one, whether it's about what job to take or how to invest your money. Always use all of the information available to you, take the time you need to make each decision, and never let your emotions cloud your judgment.

As with any big project, it's always best to start by looking at the big picture and then focus on the specifics. In terms of getting to know yourself as a person, the remaining portion of this chapter will ask you some pretty detailed questions about yourself as you embark on setting a plan for yourself to achieve overall success in your life.

The title of this book was chosen for a reason. *Your Career: Coach Yourself to Success* will give you the information you need to make intelligent decisions; however, the decisions you make are ultimately your own, because they will have an impact on you and those close to you.

Just as athletes have coaches who offer them guidance, training, and motivation, as a working professional, there's no reason why you too can't have a coach. However, just as in sports, a coach can't force an athlete to excel. If you want to achieve success, you'll need to take action and responsibility for yourself.

While it's perfectly acceptable to seek out guidance, support, and help from others, one of the biggest mistakes people make is becoming too reliant on other people. While you may occasionally receive support or help from others when it comes to achieving your goals, consider this help a bonus. Ultimately, it will be you and you alone that will determine to what degree you're able to achieve your objectives.

WHAT HAVE YOU DONE WITH YOUR LIFE UP UNTIL NOW?

Take a look at your life up until now. What are you the most proud of in terms of your accomplishments? With what aspects of yourself are you disappointed? Divide up your entire life into two main areas—personal and professional, and then answer the following questions that relate to your personal life using complete sentences.

WHERE ARE YOU NOW . . . PERSONALLY?

For the time being, forget about your professional life and focus exclusively on who you are outside of work. Think about yourself, your family, friends, personal ideals, values, and preferences as you answer the following questions. Remember, be honest with yourself as you write out your responses to these questions. Don't write answers you think you're supposed to write or that are politically correct. The purpose of this exercise is to help you do an honest self-assessment. For now, forget about your ego and what others might think.

What are the five things about yourself of which you're the most proud?

1. _____
2. _____
3. _____
4. _____
5. _____

What do you value most about your life?

_____

_____

_____

_____

_____

Who are the people closest to you? _____

_____

_____

_____

_____

Who are your best friends or the people you rely on the most?

_____

_____

_____

_____

With whom do you enjoy spending your free time?

_____

_____

_____

_____

Aside from work, what do you enjoy doing in your free time?

_____

_____

_____

_____

What are your hobbies? _____

_____

_____

_____

What charity groups, social clubs, organizations, or community groups do you currently participate in or belong to?

_____

_____

_____

_____

Why are you a participant in these groups? _____

_____

_____

_____

_____

How are the goals and values of these groups in line with your overall personal goals and ambitions? What are the similarities and differences? _____

_____

_____

_____

_____

How would you describe your personality? _____

_____

_____

_____

_____

What is it that people like most about you? _____

_____

_____

_____

_____

What do people like the least about you? _____

_____

_____

_____

_____

How do you think your friends, coworkers, and relatives describe
you? _____

_____

_____

_____

_____

What do people say about you behind your back? _____

_____

_____

_____

What do you like the most about yourself?_____

_____

_____

_____

_____

What do you like the least about yourself? _____

_____

_____

_____

_____

What is your biggest insecurity? _____

_____

_____

_____

_____

With which aspects of your appearance are you happy?

_____

_____

_____

_____

Which aspects of your appearance do you think need improvement?

_____

_____

_____

_____

When it comes to written and verbal communication, are you content with your skills? Are they developed enough? How could you improve upon these skills?

_____

_____

_____

_____

In your life right now, what are your biggest fears and concerns?

_____

_____

_____

_____

Who or what in your personal life causes you the most stress or grief? _____

_____

_____

_____

_____

Who or what in your personal life brings you the most pleasure?

_____

_____

_____

_____

If you could spend your time doing any activity, what would it be?

_____

_____

_____

_____

What are five (5) activities that you'd like to participate in, but never have?

1. _____
2. _____
3. _____
4. _____
5. _____

What has kept you from experiencing each of these activities?

_____

_____

_____

_____

When you were in school, what were your favorite subjects?

_____

_____

_____

_____

When you were in school, what were your strongest subjects?

_____

_____

_____

What are your three worst habits?

1. _____

2. _____

3. _____

Why do you have these habits? What causes them?

_____

_____

_____

_____

What could be done to eliminate these negative habits?

_____

_____

_____

_____

What has been the single best or most memorable experience of your life?

_____

_____

_____

What made this experience so special?

_____

_____

_____

_____

What could you do to make other events in your life just as special or meaningful?

_____

_____

_____

_____

What is your most prized possession? Why is it so valuable to you?

_____

_____

_____

_____

Based on your life right now, what other things do you value? (Keep in mind, your marriage or a close relationship can be of great emotional or sentimental value. Your choices don't have to be based on material objects or money.)

_____

_____

_____

_____

If you could change one thing about your life, what would it be? Why?

_____

_____

_____

_____

What is the best thing about the personal relationship(s) you currently have with loved ones? (Include your spouse, family members, boyfriend, girlfriend, etc.)

_____

_____

_____

_____

What's lacking in these relationships?

_____

_____

_____

_____

What could be done, starting today, to improve upon these relation-ships? _____

_____

_____

_____

_____

Are there any additional personal relationships you'd like to devel-op in the near future? _____

_____

_____

_____

What steps are you taking, or could you begin taking, to develop these new relationships?_____

_____

_____

_____

Describe your current living conditions and overall standard of living: _____

_____

_____

_____

_____

What could be improved upon in regard to your living conditions or standard of living? _____

_____

_____

_____

_____

What can be done in order to make it possible for you to make these improvements?_____

_____

_____

_____

_____

Describe your personal financial situation: _____

_____

_____

How has your personal financial situation changed in the past year?

_____

_____

What could be done to improve your personal financial situation over the next 12 months? _____

_____

_____

_____

_____

UNDERSTANDING YOUR PRESENT SITUATION

The answers you provided to the previous questions should have helped you develop a better understanding of who you are as a person right now. Based on what you've discovered, consider what you're the happiest about in your personal life. Also, what areas of your life need work?

For now, focus only on personal issues, such as:

- Your relationships
- Who you are as a person (based upon your own perception and the perception of others)
- Your values

- Your personality
- Your current living conditions

Now is the time to become a little critical of your answers. Are you proud of the honest responses you provided? If someone close to you were to read your responses, what would they think about you? Take some time and evaluate your personal weaknesses and insecurities. Being as specific and as detailed as possible, answer the following questions:

What needs to be improved about your life? _____

_____

_____

_____

_____

What specific strengths can you use to overcome the negative aspects of your life?   _____

_____

_____

_____

_____

What obstacles are keeping you from overcoming the negative aspects of your life? _____

_____

_____

_____

_____

What can you start doing today to overcome the negative aspects of your life?   _____

_____

_____

_____

_____

What role does your job or career play in the aspects of your personal life with which you're not happy? _____

_____

_____

_____

_____

Is there any person in your life that's holding you back from reaching your true potential? If so, what is this person doing (specifically) to hold you back? _____

_____

_____

_____

DEFINING YOUR GOALS

No matter who you are, how successful you've already become, how well educated you are, or what type of personality you have, developing specific goals and constantly working toward achieving those goals are among the key ingredients for success. As you define what your personal, professional and financial goals are, make sure that the goals are in fact your own, and that they're not being imposed on you by other people.

Sure, your parents, spouse, friends, or other relatives may encourage you or push you toward certain achievements. However, it's important that the goals you choose to pursue are your own and that they are things you truly want to accomplish for yourself. At times, the pressure that will be put on you by other people, such as a parent who wants you to follow in his or her footsteps, can be intense and even overwhelming. To achieve happiness and success in the long term, however, your actions and decisions must be your own. Of course, utilizing the advice, support, and motivation from others is definitely acceptable and encouraged.

Based upon where you are in your life right now, write down specific goals you have for yourself in the following three areas—

personal, professional, and financial. To keep things simple, consider a short-term goal as something you want to achieve within the next 12 months. A long-term goal is something that will take over one year to achieve.

As you write out your goals, make sure they're realistic. For example, if you're earning a comfortable living as a Certified Public Accountant but you've decided that your goal is to design and build fine furniture, you'll need to be very realistic about the financial sacrifice you'll be making, at least in the short term, and the difficulties you might encounter by following this less traditional career path. Being realistic will help you focus your efforts and give your dreams a solid foundation that you can use to build your success.

A realistic appraisal of the risks, effort required, and chances of success may cause you to re-evaluate some overly ambitious goals. Always make sure that your goals can be met with an amount of risk and effort with which you are comfortable.

The next few sections ask you several series of questions that will help you define your goals. When answering the questions, take some time to brainstorm on a separate piece of paper (or on a separate document in your computer) and then record your answers in this book. Keep in mind what you learned earlier in the chapter, such as the areas of your life that you would like to improve. Write down everything that comes to mind and then go over the entire list to select those items on which you would really like to focus.

Personal Goals

Personal goals deal primarily with self-improvement, relationships, and family issues. An example of a short-term personal goal might be to clean and organize your entire house within the next two weeks, or to meet five new people during the next month whom you'd consider dating in order to expand your social life.

An example of a long-term personal goal might be to get married and to have children within the next five to eight years, or to move out of your parents' house and get your own apartment within the next year.

Short-Term Personal Goals

_____

_____

_____

_____

Long-Term Personal Goals

_____

_____

_____

_____

Professional Goals

Professional goals pertain to career or job-related issues. An example of a short-term professional goal might be to find and land a first job (by the time you graduate from school). A short-term career-related goal might also be to earn a raise or promotion within the next year, or to ace your next quarterly employee evaluation.

An example of a long-term career goal might be to move up the corporate ladder where you're currently employed and ultimately become a senior vice president within the next three to five years.

Short-Term Professional Goals

_____

_____

_____

_____

_____

Long-Term Professional Goals

_____

_____

_____

_____

Financial Goals

As the title suggests, financial goals have to do with money, investments and assets. An example of a short-term financial goal might
be to pay off your credit card debt within the next eight months. A
long-term financial goal might be to acquire a personal net worth of
$300,000 dollars by the time you reach age 45, or to build up a
stock/investment portfolio worth of over $100,000 within the next
four years.

Short-Term Financial Goals   _____

_____

_____

_____

_____

Long-Term Financial Goals   _____

_____

_____

_____

_____

HOW CAREER AND FINANCIAL GOALS FIT INTO
YOUR PERSONAL LIFE

If you're unmarried, have no children, and you don't have to support
anyone but yourself, it's very easy to make career-related decisions,

to dedicate your life (at least for a while) to your career, and to take career-related risks. Achieving a balance between your personal and professional life isn't as critical, and it's okay if your work takes precedence in your life.

However, once you get involved in a serious romantic relationship, get married, have children, or take on supporting your parents in their old age, for example, the career-related decisions you make will have an impact on your life, as well as the lives of people close to you.

For example, your employer might offer you an incredible promotion and raise; however, to accept it would require relocating to another state. With no family ties, this decision would be a lot easier to make than if you have to worry about your spouse leaving his or her job, and pulling your kids out of their school.

The career goals you set should be in line with what's strategically possible based on your personal situation. If your career-related goal is to eventually become a top-level executive within the company you currently work for, but in order to do this, you'll need to return to school either part-time or full-time to earn an MBA, for example, you'll have to consider how this education will be paid for, whether or not you have the time to attend classes and study, and what impact returning to school and juggling a full-time job will have on your family.

Likewise, if you're a woman who is considering having children within the next few years, you'll need to decide early on what role your career will play in your life during and after your pregnancy. Are you willing to give up your career and be a stay-at-home mom? Will you return to work part-time? Will you hire a nanny and return to work full-time within weeks after giving birth? What impact will each of these scenarios have on your personal and professional life?

Every career-related decision you make will have a short- and long-term impact on you and those close to you. If you're totally dedicated to achieving your goals, you can make them a reality. It's critical, however, to understand what you're getting into and determine what sacrifices you'll need to make in order to juggle your personal and professional life.

Consider how every career-related goal you write down will

potentially impact your personal goals and financial goals, and how each set of goals interrelate. Chances are, your career and financial-related goals will integrate closely. For example, if you want to buy yourself a $2.5 million home in the next five years, and to do this, you must work your way from being a manager to a vice president within your company, you'll need to adjust your career-related goals in order to eventually achieve your financial goal.

In subsequent chapters, you'll discover how to go about setting short-term and long-term goals and then divide up those goals into smaller, easily achievable goals. You'll learn how to develop an organized approach to achieving your goals, discover tips for staying focused and motivated, plus learn how to track and measure your successes.

One of the keys to being able to achieve goals is to constantly evaluate what your goals are and be ready to modify them as unexpected events happen in your life. At times, things might go better than planned. In some situations, you may face and have to deal with unexpected obstacles. There may also be times when you find a change in focus will lead to better results.

As you get older, your priorities and values will change. You will become more mature and your outlook on life will be altered as you obtain additional life experience. For these reasons, you always want to keep an open mind as you're confronted with new and exciting opportunities that may require you to alter your goals and objectives.

By the time you're done reading this book, there's a good chance you'll want to return to the goal-related questions you responded to in the previous section of this chapter and rework or modify some or all of your answers. You may discover that your personal happiness and the ability to work at a job that you truly love (even if it's for less pay) is well worth pursuing, even if it means your long-term financial goals may no longer be achievable in the time frame you've outlined.

You may discover five years from now that the career path you've selected really isn't right for you, and that you'd prefer to return to school to earn a different degree, and then pursue an entirely different career opportunity in an unrelated field or different industry altogether.

As you're forced to make important, potentially life-changing decisions, whether they relate to your career, finances or personal life, never make these decisions rashly and never lose focus on whatever it is you're trying to accomplish in the long-term. Always remember that short-term sacrifices may be a necessity, and that there are seldom any shortcuts to achieving success.

CREATING A PERSONALIZED, GOAL-ACHIEVEMENT ACTION PLAN

Earlier in this chapter you were asked to define what you currently perceive your short- and long-term personal, professional, and financial goals to be. Hopefully, you listed specific goals. Simply listing your goals in writing and referring to them often (on a daily basis, if possible), is a major step toward being able to achieve those goals.

Especially to accomplish your long-term goals, however, you'll need to devise a detailed action plan for each goal as well as a timeline. As you'll soon learn in Chapter 5, one of the first steps in achieving your primary long-term goals is to divide each of them up into a series of smaller, more achievable short-term goals, and then to create a timeline for achieving each of those smaller goals.

Once you set out to define and begin achieving your goals, this becomes an ongoing process that requires commitment, hard work, and dedication on your part. You must focus your energies and then stay focused until your objectives are completed. At times, this won't be an easy process, so one of the challenges you'll face is staying motivated.

The action plan you devise for achieving your goals must be personalized to meet your own needs, lifestyle, and personality. You never want to take on too much, or you'll quickly find yourself overwhelmed and frustrated. Likewise, you always want to be challenged in order to maintain your interest and motivation.

In order to succeed, you'll have to determine, over time, what your personal limits are, in terms of what you can handle emotionally and

physically, and adjust your action plan accordingly. Most importantly, you must never be afraid to fail.

When it comes to making life-changing decisions and taking steps
to improve your career, personal life, or financial well being, be prepared to make mistakes, but at the same time, always learn from
those mistakes and never repeat them. If you make a mistake, don't
look at it as a personal failure and get depressed. Instead, consider
it a valuable learning experience. What would you do differently
next time? What can be done to fix the situation now that the mistake has been made? What lessons were learned from the mistake?
In the future, how can you (and how will you) benefit from the
knowledge you have acquired? What can be done to insure that a
similar mistake never happens again?

While hard work and dedication will play major roles in your
ability to achieve long-term success, no matter what your goals are,
your attitude and personality will also be integral factors.
Developing and maintaining a positive attitude is important, as is
learning how to work well with others so that the people you work
or interact with (personally or professionally) like and respect you.

Once you set your mind to achieving the things you've listed as
your goals, invest the necessary time to create a detailed action plan
(a step-by-step plan to meet your goals) so that you always know
what needs to be done next in order to achieve your objectives.
Action plans are discussed in great detail in Chapter 5, and are an
essential step in coaching yourself to success.

Finally, always pay attention to yourself and who you are as a
person. Never compromise what you believe to be moral and right
simply to make someone else happy or to achieve a goal. Make sure
that the way you are accomplishing your goals enhances who you
are, and doesn't detract from your sense of self-worth. For example,
if you are presented with the opportunity to take the credit for someone else's work, even though this might earn you a promotion, you
will undermine your success because you have compromised your
character. There's always a right way and a wrong way of accomplishing something. The wrong way might save you time, money,

and maybe even some frustration, but in the long term, always strive to be the best person you can be.

The power to succeed is within you. Your hopes, dreams, and desires can all become reality. You can make positive things happen for yourself if you're willing to take control over your own life and your actions. It's within your power to avoid getting stuck in a bad marriage or relationship, and to avoid getting stuck in a dead-end job. If you're already in a bad situation, with the proper guidance and internal drive, you can vastly improve and/or drastically alter the situation you're currently in.

You've already taken the right first step by purchasing and reading this book. If you've answered the questions posed in this chapter, you have also already begun developing a truer understanding of who you are as a person. As you proceed to the next chapter, a focus on your career and professional life will begin.

C H A P T E R 2

getting to know your
professional self

SO, HOW'S IT going so far? Does your hand hurt from writing out answers to all of the questions posed to you in the previous chapter? While you live with yourself 24 hours per day, everyday, few people are truly and totally honest with themselves when it comes to evaluating whom they are, what they believe in, what's important to them, and what their values are. The questions in the previous chapter were posed to help you discover a better understanding of yourself as a person.

In this chapter, you will be asked another series of questions. This time, the objective is to develop an understanding of your professional interests and aspirations. When it comes to work and your career:

- What are your likes and dislikes?
- What are your goals and aspirations?
- What will it take to transform yourself into someone who is excited to wake up each and every morning and go to work?
- What are your passions?
- What skills do you possess right now that make you a valuable employee?
- How can you make yourself more marketable in today's competitive job market?

These are some of the bigger questions to which this chapter will help you uncover answers. To do this, invest some additional time and answer the following questions using complete sentences. Once again, it's necessary for you to be totally honest with yourself. The answers you provide to these questions will help you determine what type of career opportunities you should pursue, based on your skills, interests, and desires.

From these questions, you'll also be able to ascertain what your long-term career goals and professional dreams are. Later, with this information, you'll be able to develop an action plan for transforming your goals and dreams into reality.

Obviously, just because you write something down, it doesn't mean that what you put on paper will ultimately come true. This is only the first step in a long process that involves hard work, drive, determination, motivation, knowledge, and dedication.

This process will start, however, with you determining what you want out of your professional life. From there, you can create a road map for yourself and put yourself on a career path designed to make your objectives achievable.

UNDERSTANDING YOUR PROFESSIONAL SELF

As you respond to the following questions, think about what you learned from the previous chapter about yourself as a person. Also, keep in mind that there's no need to share your answers with other

people. You will, however, want to incorporate some of the information you include within your responses into your job search
efforts, your resume, and in the formulation of your career-related
goals.

What job title or position do you currently fill or are you qualified to
fill? _____

_____

_____

_____

What alternate job titles are you qualified to fill? _____

_____

_____

_____

_____

What is your greatest career-related achievement? How can you
document this achievement to potential employers?_____

_____

_____

_____

_____

While in school, what were three of your most impressive accomplishments, achievements and/or awards? _____

_____

_____

_____

_____

What is your single most marketable professional or work-related
skill? Why? _____

_____

_____

_____

What is the most impressive result or success you've achieved on the job using this skill? _____

_____

_____

_____

_____

What five other skills do you possess that are the most useful in the work you do now (or plan to do in the near future)?

1. _____

2. _____

3. _____

4. _____

5. _____

List specific examples of how you have used each of these skills at work. What was accomplished as a result?

Skill: _____   Result: _____

Skill: _____   Result: _____

Skill: _____   Result: _____

Skill: _____   Result: _____

Skill: _____   Result: _____

What keywords or industry buzzwords can be used to describe each of your skill(s)?

_____

_____

_____

_____

What are one or two things about you as a professional that sets you apart from other people working in your field? What makes you special? _____

_____

_____

_____

What professional or personal skills do you currently lack?

_____

_____

_____

_____

If you possessed these skills, how would it benefit your career?

_____

_____

_____

_____

What would it take to obtain the skills that you currently lack?

_____

_____

_____

_____

What skills do you have that require improvement to make you more proficient? _____

_____

_____

_____

_____

In what time frame could you realistically obtain the necessary training?_____

_____

_____

_____

Looking at your career thus far, what has been your favorite job and place to work? Why? _____

_____

_____

_____

Based on your current skills and qualifications, write a job description for what you perceive to be a desirable job. Make sure this is a job you could apply for (if it were available) and potentially receive today.

_____

_____

_____

_____

How does your current job differ from your dream job?

_____

_____

_____

_____

What would be your ultimate dream job? Create a job description for that job. (For the time being, don't worry about whether or not you're qualified for this job, but make sure it is one that could potentially exist.)

_____

_____

_____

_____

In what type of work environment would you like to be employed? (A large corporation, a small business, a home-based business, a company with over 100 employees, a company with under 10 employees, etc.)

_____

_____

_____

_____

What type of people would you like as your coworkers? (Describe these people in terms of their age, interests, qualifications, personalities, etc.) _____

_____

_____

_____

_____

What type of work schedule would you like to have, or would you prosper the most in if you maintained? (Part-time, full-time, 9 A.M. to 5 P.M., etc.) _____

_____

_____

_____

What work-related tasks do you most enjoy doing?

_____

_____

_____

_____

What work-related tasks do you least enjoy?

_____

_____

_____

_____

At which work-related tasks are you the most proficient?

_____

_____

_____

_____

What work-related tasks are you responsible for, at which you do not excel? _____

_____

_____

_____

_____

Describe your professional career path as it stands right now? Where are you today, and where are you headed?

_____

_____

_____

_____

If you could alter this career path and improve upon it, what would change? _____

_____

_____

_____

_____

What aspects of your work make you the happiest? What do you most look forward to?

_____

_____

_____

_____

With minor changes, what aspects of your professional life could make you happy or excited?

_____

_____

_____

_____

What aspects of your work do you enjoy the least? Is there anything about your current employment situation that makes you miserable? If so, what? _____

_____

_____

_____

_____

How would you describe your professional attitude?

_____

_____

_____

_____

How do you believe your coworkers describe your professional attitude and personality? What about your superiors?

_____

_____

_____

_____

If you were to pursue additional education or professional training, what would you study and why? How would this potentially help your career?

_____

_____

_____

_____

When it comes to work-related benefits and perks, what's important to you? (Examples might include: health insurance, stock options, daycare, flexible work schedule, etc.)

_____

_____

_____

When you're recognized for doing a good job at work, how do you like to be rewarded?

_____

_____

_____

_____

What five qualities about a new job opportunity would you look for, based on the answers you provided to the previous questions in this section? For example, would you look for a full-time job in a large corporation, where your co-workers were around your age and your daily work-related responsibilities included things you enjoy doing? Be specific in terms of what you'd look for in a future employment situation.

1. _____
2. _____
3. _____
4. _____
5. _____

What is currently holding you back from obtaining what you perceive to be your dream job?

_____

_____

_____

_____

What would it take, starting today, to overcome these obstacles?

_____

_____

_____

_____

How would you rate your skills in the following areas? Use the following key to help you rate your level of proficiency.

1 = Non-Existent, 2 = Needs Work, 3 = Average, 4 = Excellent

Written communication skills:	1	2	3	4
Verbal communication skills:	1	2	3	4
Public speaking skills:	1	2	3	4
Listening skills:	1	2	3	4
Reading skills:	1	2	3	4
Computer literacy skills:	1	2	3	4
Time management skills:	1	2	3	4
Organizational skills:	1	2	3	4
Managerial/leadership skills:	1	2	3	4
Interpersonal skills:	1	2	3	4

For the skills you rated as being "non-existent," "needs work," or "average," how important are they for the job you currently have? What about for your dream job?

Written communication skills
    Current Job: Important   Not Critical
    Dream Job: Important   Not Critical
Verbal communication skills
    Current Job: Important   Not Critical
    Dream Job: Important   Not Critical
Public speaking skills
    Current Job: Important   Not Critical
    Dream Job: Important   Not Critical
Listening skills
    Current Job: Important   Not Critical
    Dream Job: Important   Not Critical
Reading skills
    Current Job: Important   Not Critical
    Dream Job: Important   Not Critical

Computer literacy skills

Current Job:	Important	Not Critical
Dream Job:	Important	Not Critical

Time management skills

Current Job:	Important	Not Critical
Dream Job:	Important	Not Critical

Organizational skills

Current Job:	Important	Not Critical
Dream Job:	Important	Not Critical

Managerial/leadership skills

Current Job:	Important	Not Critical
Dream Job:	Important	Not Critical

Interpersonal skills

Current Job:	Important	Not Critical
Dream Job:	Important	Not Critical

What can you do, starting today, to begin learning or improving each of these skill areas? (For example: on the job training, night classes, weekend classes, books on tape, videocassette courses, online distance learning, reading training manuals, etc.)

_____

_____

_____

_____

If you were to apply for your ultimate dream job right now, what reason(s) would the employer give for not hiring you? What skills, experience, or education are you lacking?

_____

_____

_____

_____

Based on your current career path, what promotions or job changes would you have to make over time in order to ultimately land your dream job? What would be the anticipated timeline for each of these career-related steps?

_____

_____

_____

_____

Right now, out of every 24-hour day and 168-hour week, what percentage of time do you spend:

	PER DAY	PER WEEK
On the job (at work)	_____ %	_____ %
Doing work-related tasks at home	_____ %	_____ %
Pursuing new skills, education, or knowledge	_____ %	_____ %
Doing something physical that's healthy	_____ %	_____ %
Doing something that you enjoy and that's fun	_____ %	_____ %
Spending quality time with family and close friends	_____ %	_____ %
Doing something that's spiritual	_____ %	_____ %

In a perfect world, how would you adjust these percentages (being realistic) in order to make your life happier? More productive? More personally fulfilling? More emotionally fulfilling? More spiritually fulfilling?

	PER DAY	PER WEEK
On the job (at work)	_____ %	_____ %
Doing work-related tasks at home	_____ %	_____ %
Pursuing new skills, education, or knowledge	_____ %	_____ %
Doing something physical that's healthy	_____ %	_____ %

Doing something that you enjoy and that's fun	_____%	_____%
Spending quality time with family and close friends	_____%	_____%
Doing something that's spiritual	_____%	_____%

Based on the way you answered all of these questions, you should now have a pretty good understanding of what type(s) of things you're good at, what you enjoy, what your professional aspirations are, and what types of job(s) you'd like to pursue.

You should also have come to some conclusions about what type of work environment you'd be most productive in, what type of work would make you the happiest, what skills you currently have that you're using to move your career forward, and what skills you still need to develop in order to achieve your professional goals.

If you answered all these questions in one sitting, you're probably pretty tired. As you take a break, think about all of the answers you've committed to paper thus far that relate to your personal and professional life. Think about where you are now in your life and in your career, and where you'd ultimately like to be.

YOU ARE WHAT YOU DO, OR ARE YOU?

For most people, their job becomes an integral part of their life, whether it's intentional or not. Many people spend at least eight hours per day on the job, and then wind up bringing the pleasures or stresses of work home with them. The quality of your work life will invariably influence your personal life, and one important ingredient to creating success is finding the right balance between your work and personal life so that you can achieve your career, financial, and personal goals without sacrificing one for the other.

Generally speaking, people who love their work don't mind if their work becomes a way of life to which they dedicate themselves. This is often something that comes naturally. People who have managed to pinpoint an occupation or job at which they excel and that they enjoy doing are often the people who are dedicated to their careers. They're willing to work hard and enjoy devoting themselves to their ongoing success.

Everyone has a chance to choose his or her own professional destiny . . . even you. You can choose to accept job offers and career opportunities that you'll enjoy, in which you'll prosper, and that offer future advancement opportunities, or you can choose to accept dead-end, non-challenging jobs, simply to earn a paycheck.

Sometime these choices are not easy. Turning against the wishes of a parent, for example, and not following in their professional footsteps can be a source of conflict. However, if making that decision means the difference between getting stuck in a career that isn't personally rewarding and pursuing a career that you love, you must choose to follow your own heart and be happy.

What you choose to do with your professional life will play a major role in defining who you are as a person, how you dress, who your friends and professional acquaintances are, and what type of lifestyle you'll be able to lead. The amount of free time you have will most likely be dictated by your job (at least in terms of your vacation schedule and daily work schedule), and it may even influence *how* you spend your free time.

While it's easy to get caught up in the rat race of a career, learning how to balance your professional life and personal life (and making sure you actually have some form of personal life) will go a long way toward ensuring your long-term happiness and emotional well being. Developing time-management skills, organizational skills, and the ability to leave the stresses associated with work at the office are all useful in developing a healthy balance between your personal and professional life.

Failure to create this balance could transform you into someone who lives for his or her work—and only his or her work. If you're married, in a relationship, have children or other people who are close to you, becoming overly involved in your work can take an incredibly negative toll on those relationships. If you live alone, becoming all consumed in your work will certainly help you move your career forward faster. However, giving up a personal life, even for a while, can be a major sacrifice that could easily prevent you from fulfilling your long-term personal goals.

As you define your professional and financial goals, keep your personal goals in mind. For example, if you accept a job that will move your career forward quickly, but that requires you to travel nine months out of the year, it will be extremely difficult to cultivate a personal relationship. If one of your personal goals is eventually to meet someone and get married, a job that requires a great deal of travel might not be the right choice for you.

Developing a reputation for being highly motivated and career driven can be a positive thing; however, when it comes to planning out your life, you probably don't want your life and your career to be one and the same—at least over the long term. Again, this all has to do with making personal and professional decisions and how you choose to pursue your various goals.

There's a flipside, however. When was the last time you walked into a retail store, convenience store, doctor's office, or supermarket, for example, and expected to receive friendly service from the person behind the counter, but instead, you wound up being ignored or treated rudely? Chances are, this treatment comes from someone who has made poor career decisions, yet he or she is unwilling or unmotivated to make the necessary changes to improve their professional life.

Dissatisfaction with your work life can have very serious personal consequences. If your time at work is a source of frustration, boredom, or other negative emotions, it can lead to feelings of depression that can impact every other aspect of your life. However, if you recognize that your unhappiness at work is having a negative effect on your personal life, you've already made an important step in turning the situation around.

A positive career path can become a dominating and all-consuming force in your life, where your desire to succeed is so great that you forsake your personal life. Likewise, a negative employment situation can spill over into your personal life and dominate your whole outlook. One key to success is developing a balance between your personal and professional life.

SPELLING OUT YOUR PROFESSIONAL GOALS
AND OBJECTIVES

Based on all the questions you've answered thus far, all the professional work experience you've had in your career to date, and what your personal preferences, hopes, goals and dreams are, now is the time to develop a specific plan for your life that contains short- and long-term personal, financial, and professional goals.

In this chapter, the focus is on developing professional goals, along with learning how to find job opportunities in which you'll prosper and enjoy. Consider exactly where you are right now in terms of your career. What did it take to get to this point? What have you learned so far about how the business world operates?

Where do you want to be six months down the road? One year from now? Five years from now? Ten years from now? What are your plans for retirement? Before you can find and accept your next career opportunity, consider each of these questions and determine if the job you're about to accept will help you move forward in your career and achieve what you want in the future.

When it comes to following a career path, each promotion you receive, each job transfer you accept, and each new job or career opportunity you take on can have one of three results:

1. It can help move your career forward, providing you with additional knowledge, experience, and skills that make you a more valuable employee. The job can be a metaphorical steppingstone to get you to where you ultimately want to be in your professional life. You know that once you master this new job, you'll receive a promotion or be qualified to fill a better job that requires additional skills and has better financial rewards.
2. It can be a lateral career move, that doesn't necessarily move your career forward but might offer some benefits. For example, a person who worked as a cashier at a

clothing retail store in the mall might decide to obtain a similar job at a pet store because she has an interest in animals. While she might have similar responsibilities and the same rate of pay, this lateral career move might allow her to move closer to her dream of someday working for a veterinarian. A lateral career move is a sort of sidestep that might help you change the course of your career.

3. It can stall your career. The job offers no additional training, no chances for earning promotions and climbing the corporate ladder, and no future potential that could help you forward your career. In other words, what you're doing today on the job is exactly what you'll be doing next month, next year and as long as you hold the same position.

From the questionnaire in this chapter, you basically now know what type of employment situation would be considered a "dream job," based on things like:

- What your qualifications are
- What your most marketable skills are
- Your greatest strengths
- What work-related responsibilities you enjoy
- What type of work environment in which you'd most likely prosper
- What you liked most about previous work experiences
- What you like least about previous work experience
- What type of people you'd prefer to have as your coworkers

Armed with this knowledge, spend some time thinking carefully about what you'd like your long-term professional goals to be. Ask yourself what the overall purpose of your professional life is. What do you ultimately want the outcome of your professional life to be?

Using as much detail as possible, define the underlining purpose of your professional life:

_____

_____

_____

_____

Using as much detail as possible, describe what you want the long-term outcome of your professional life to be:

_____

_____

_____

_____

DEFINING YOUR FINANCIAL GOALS

There's a saying, "money can't buy you happiness," and that's probably true; however, having money can certainly open up many doors of opportunity in both your personal and professional life. While you may never become a multi-millionaire, you can learn to maximize the financial resources you have available.

Thus far in _Your Career: Coach Yourself to Success_, you've answered questions to help you define and achieve your personal and professional goals. In this section, you'll be asked a series of questions that will help you define your long-term financial goals. While your financial goals will often be closely related to your personal and professional goals, these should be defined separately.

Knowing your current lifestyle and what your daily, weekly, or monthly expenses are, if you were to change jobs tomorrow, you should have a pretty good idea of what your compensation package must include in order for you to maintain your standard of living.

As you set out to find and land a new job, set financial goals for yourself. These goals might include starting the new job with a 10% salary increase (providing you're qualified to earn it). You might also want to seek a job that will offer you the opportunity to earn raises or promotions, so you can increase your earning potential by 30, 40, or 50% over the next five years, for example.

You'll want to establish financial goals that will allow you to achieve your personal goals. For example, if one of your personal goals is to own a 40-foot sailboat in the next five years, you'll require money to purchase and maintain the boat. In order to achieve this goal, one of your financial goals will need to include earning or saving enough money for this rather significant expense. To achieve the financial goal of being able to pay for your boat, you may need to set up an ongoing savings or investment plan, learn how to better manage your money, and/or find ways of earning additional money. These potential financial goals and action plans can be created in conjunction with your personal goals.

Likewise, if your professional goal is to become a senior vice president of a Fortune 500 corporation or to someday own your own business, reaching this level of professional success will most likely include earning a significant salary. Thus, your financial resources will be greater, which means properly managing your finances will become a more serious responsibility. Discovering what do to with your money and how to manage it will require you to set additional financial goals for yourself.

The following questions will help you define your financial goals and spending habits.

Including salary, benefits, investments, etc., how much money do you earn right now?

_____

How would you describe your spending habits? Saving habits? Investment habits? _____

_____

_____

_____

How would you describe your overall standard of living?

_____

_____

_____

_____

Do you have a monthly personal budget in place? (Spell out what your budget includes and how significant portions of your income are spent. Include expanded costs such as housing, transportation, food, insurance, leisure expenses, etc.)_____

_____

_____

_____

_____

Does your income easily allow you to sustain your current standard of living? _____

_____

_____

_____

How reliant are you on credit cards and other loans? What could be done to reduce this reliance?

_____

_____

_____

Over the next 12 months, how would you like your standard of living to change? _____

_____

_____

_____

_____

How much additional money will be required to adjust your standard of living from where it is now to where you want it to be in 12 months?

_____

_____

_____

_____

Over the next three to five years, how would you like your standard of living to change?

_____

_____

_____

_____

How much additional money will be required to adjust your standard of living from where it is now, to where you want it to be in three to five years?

_____

_____

_____

_____

Define your long-term financial goal(s):

_____

_____

_____

_____

What can you do to enhance your earning potential now and in the future?

_____

_____

_____

Do you have a financial plan in place for long-term savings and investment? _____

_____

_____

_____

In the future, what type(s) of large expenses do you anticipate having? (For example, buying a house, buying/leasing a new car, raising children, college tuition for children, supporting your aging parents, dealing with a long-term illness, or taking a vacation.)

_____

_____

_____

_____

What plans do you already have in place that will allow you to afford these significant expenses?

_____

_____

_____

_____

What plans still need to be put in place so you'll be able to afford your anticipated future expenses?

_____

_____

_____

_____

What are you doing right now to plan for your retirement?

_____

_____

_____

_____

What additional financial plans need to be implemented to allow for a comfortable retirement?

_____

_____

_____

_____

Are you comfortable managing your own finances? If not, how could a working with a certified financial planner or accountant be beneficial? _____

_____

_____

_____

_____

Knowing your personal spending habits, what do you need to change in order to achieve your financial goals?

_____

_____

_____

_____

In terms of your own personal value system, how important is money? _____

_____

_____

_____

_____

What percentage of your income is donated to charity?

_____

In the future, how would you like this percentage to change?

_____

_____

_____

Will the financial goals you have in place for yourself allow you to achieve your long-term personal goals? If not, what needs to be altered? _____

_____

_____

_____

_____

Are your financial goals realistic, based on your current earning potential and qualifications (and what you believe your earning potential will be in the future)? _____

_____

_____

Based on your current budget and standard of living, if you were to accept a new job tomorrow, what type of compensation package would you require to maintain your standard of living and possibly improve upon it immediately? _____

_____

_____

_____

What additional employee benefits or perks are or will be important to you?

_____

_____

_____

_____

Over the next 12 months, three years, five years, and ten years, what do you anticipate your financial needs to be in terms of salary and overall compensation (either from your current or a future employer)?

_____

_____

_____

_____

What needs to be done to insure you'll receive the financial compensation you know you'll require either to maintain or improve upon your standard of living in the future?

_____

_____

_____

_____

What additional financial knowledge do you need to better manage your finances and investments?

_____

_____

_____

_____

How and where can this knowledge be obtained? What can you begin doing immediately to begin acquiring this knowledge?

_____

_____

_____

_____

DIVIDING UP YOUR GOALS AND MAKING THEM ACHIEVABLE

As you live your life from this point on, never lose sight of the outcome you want to achieve. Right now, that outcome might seem like it's light years away and almost impossible to achieve, but, as you'll soon discover, by taking that giant long-term goal and intelligently dividing it up into a series of smaller, short-term goals, all of which allow you to constantly work toward your one long-term objective, things become far more manageable.

Without losing sight of what your purpose is and what you want the outcome to be, start to determine, based on what your current situation is right now, what it would take to move your career just one small step forward in the next few weeks or months. Do you need to learn new skills? Work harder to earn a promotion? Ace your next employee evaluation/review? Find a new job that offers better training and the ability to move your career forward?

Start to develop an action plan for yourself that will allow you to work toward your long-term goals by accomplishing a series of short-term goals. As you do this, make sure you don't overwhelm yourself by setting too many short-term goals at once. Start off slowly. As you begin to see yourself making progress and working toward your ultimate objective, you'll discover ways of making the process happen faster, but for now, take small, manageable steps. Just make sure that everything you do moves you in a forward direction.

You should never lose sight of what you want the outcome to be. Based on unexpected events and unforeseen circumstances, you will most likely have to modify the action plan that you design to steer you toward your ultimate goal, however, while the smaller steps you take might change, the overall outcome you're looking to achieve should always remain consistent and become ingrained within your conscious and subconscious mind as something extremely positive that you're working toward.

CREATING A TIMETABLE AND ACTION PLAN

Especially when it comes to smaller, short-term goals, it's critical that you develop a timetable for achieving each of them. Set a deadline for yourself so you know exactly what needs to be accomplished and when it needs to be accomplished. This will dramatically help you schedule your day-to-day activities so that you're always moving forward toward your long-term goal.

With each smaller goal or objective that you set, determine exactly what will be involved in accomplishing it. What needs to get done? What needs to be learned? What steps need to be taken? How long will each of the steps take to accomplish? Being totally realistic, how long should it take you to achieve each short-term goal? What obstacles might you encounter? How will you deal with these obstacles and overcome them in a timely manner?

Proper planning and your ability to make well thought out and educated decisions will play a major role in your short- and long-term success. Later in this book, you'll discover how to overcome the obstacles that might prevent you from achieving success (Chapter 3), how to develop a detailed action plan based on the short-term and long-term goals you set for yourself (Chapter 5), and learn useful time management techniques (Chapter 6) that will help you become a more organized person.

MAKING YOURSELF MORE MARKETABLE RIGHT NOW

What's happening in your career right now? Are you looking to earn a promotion? Do you need to find a new job? Are you working extremely hard at your current job but not receiving the recognition or financial compensation you deserve? Are you absolutely miserable in your current employment situation?

No matter what you do for a living, chances are that with a small amount of effort on your part, you can take the education, skills, and work experience you already have and make yourself even more marketable.

It is important to present yourself as someone who will add value to the company where you work or would like to work. Position yourself as a valuable asset and someone who has the potential to become an even greater asset over time. When a company hires you as its new employee, that company is making an investment in you. Ultimately, the company expects to receive a positive return on its investment. If you're able to generate that positive result, your chances of earning a raise or promotion down the line increase dramatically.

By constantly learning new skills and taking on additional responsibilities once you're happily employed, you will continue to become an even greater asset to the company you work for. As a result, you'll be worth more and when it comes to being evaluated for a raise or promotion, you'll be able to justify the additional financial investment you want your employer to make in you.

Some of the questions you answered earlier in this chapter focused on your skills and abilities. All of these skills and abilities, combined with your education and your experience (both life experience and professional experience) contribute to your overall skill set. For the moment, let's assume that you have the core qualifications for the job you have or for which you apply.

Your mission as you progress in your career is to market yourself, your skills, education, experience, personality, and appearance as a package. You want to set yourself apart from the competition and focus on what makes you a uniquely valuable asset to an employer.

Whether you are applying for a new job or trying to excel at your current position, study the job description and/or help wanted ad that's published or distributed by the employer, determine which of your skills are best utilized to meet the responsibilities of that job. Once you pinpoint exactly what the employer is looking for in terms of core requirements for the position, make sure that you market yourself as someone with those qualifications and then some.

In addition to those core responsibilities, highlight things about yourself that add value, such as additional skills you can utilize, past work experience, or other aspects about yourself that will capture that attention of the employer. As you begin to market yourself to an employer, be prepared to support your statements with hardcore quantitative and qualitative proof.

Demonstrate that you not only have the skills required for a job, but that you know how to use them and that in past employment experiences, you have used your skills to achieve positive results (which you're prepared to document).

The best way to determine exactly what an employer is looking for, whether in a current or a new employee, is to do research. Learn as much as you can about the new company or your industry. Talk to as many people as you can who are successful in your field. Surf the Internet to gather information. When applying for a new job, pay careful attention to the job description and help wanted ad when gathering specific clues about what the company is looking for.

In addition to developing a true understanding of what the employer is looking for, it's critical that you know exactly what you're capable of offering and how much you're worth as an employee. When it comes to compensation, one excellent online resource is Salary.com (www.salary.com). This site's Salary Wizard will help you determine exactly what you're worth based on your skills, job title, and the geographic area where you work or would like to work.

The more you know about yourself and your employer, the easier it will be for you to market yourself as someone who is uniquely qualified to fill a specific job opening. This strategy works if you're looking for a new job, with a new employer, or if you're looking to earn a raise or promotion with an existing employer.

Always think in terms of adding value to what you can offer to the employer. Knowing what the employer's concerns and motivations are, you should be able to address those issues and position yourself as a qualified applicant who not only meets the core requirements for the job, but has the potential to grow professionally in the future.

While personality does play a role in whether or not you get hired, your ability to market your skills, education, and experience as a package is what will determine whether or not you get hired in most instances.

From your standpoint, once you know what the employer is looking for and you learn about the company's culture and what it expects from its employees, you must determine, for yourself, if the employment opportunity is something you'll enjoy and have an interest in pursuing. Even if the potential employer begs you to accept a job offer, if that offer doesn't fit within your career plan, you should definitely think twice about accepting it.

No matter what you do for a living, at various points in your life, you're going to face obstacles and career-related challenges. If you're unable to confront these obstacles and overcome them, you

could easily lose focus and your career's ongoing forward momentum could stall out. To keep this from happening, it's an excellent
strategy to understand the types of obstacles you might encounter
and prepare yourself in advance to cope with them head-on. This is
the focus of Chapter 3.

identifying the obstacles preventing your success

THERE'S PROBABLY A reason why you're at this point in your life, and why you haven't yet achieved your long-term personal, professional, or financial goals. Perhaps there's something, either real or perceived, that's holding you back and keeping you from reaching your ultimate potential. This chapter will explore many of the common obstacles that tend to hold people back from pursuing their dreams and achieving their goals.

As you read this chapter, think about what's holding *you* back. What's keeping you from taking the necessary actions, starting today, to achieve the things in life that you believe will make you both happy and successful. Once you've pinpointed what you believe is keeping you from achieving your goals and dreams, think about ways of confronting these obstacles head-on and overcoming them.

Never be content with simply accepting an obstacle as something that is holding you back. This negative stance means you're accepting defeat and failure, thus giving up any chance of achieving your objectives. No matter what obstacles you face (or will face in the future), chances are there are things you can do—with proper planning, additional education, hard work, dedication, and maybe the support of others—to help you overcome them.

Once you discover each of the obstacles that is blocking your ability to achieve your ultimate goal(s), create sub-goals or mini-goals for yourself that focus specifically on overcoming each obstacle. In doing this, determine what needs to be done to overcome each obstacle, divide this objective into smaller and more manageable tasks, create deadlines and a timeline for achieving your mini-goals, and then implement your action plan.

Nobody is going to tell you that overcoming your obstacles is going to be a quick and easy process—it's not. In some cases, it could take you many years to develop the skills or obtain the additional education necessary to overcome a challenge or obstacle. There may also be instances where a specific challenge can't become overcome, which means you'll have to develop alternative methods or "work arounds" for achieving the goals you've set for yourself. In these situations, your creativity will prove invaluable.

....

A learning disability, such as dyslexia, is one example of an obstacle that can't be eliminated, but can be "worked around." There are many ways of learning to compensate for learning disabilities, so that these "obstacles" do not impede success. With the proper training, tools, and resources, people with learning disabilities such as dyslexia can lead extremely successful lives, without any hindrances, both on the job and in their personal life.

....

As time goes on, chances are you're going to face a wide range of challenges and obstacles in your personal and professional life. By planning your goals and objectives, hopefully you'll be able to predict many of the challenges you'll face and in the process, develop ways of overcoming these challenges.

Life is full of surprises, however. New challenges and situations are always going to arise, and there's no way to have contingency plans in place for every possible scenario. In these situations, facing the obstacles you encounter with an open mind and a determination to succeed will help you remain focused and able to continuously work toward your objectives.

By truly understanding your talents, your skill set, and what you're trying to accomplish, you'll always be able to discover ways of utilizing your strengths and maximizing your potential for success.

POTENTIAL OBSTACLES BLOCKING YOUR SUCCESS

It's easy to look at your life and blame someone else or something that's "out of your control" for things that aren't going well in your life. Likewise, when one of your goals or objectives can't be achieved, it's easy to look at the obstacles that are in your way and blame them for your lack of success.

There are always going to be obstacles in your path; however, once you learn to confront and overcome these challenges, achieving long-term success will be much easier. Taking responsibility for your own destiny is critical for achieving success, which means no longer blaming other people for things you're unable to accomplish.

So, what types of things are holding you back from achieving your true potential and making your dreams become a reality? The following list includes some of the most common obstacles people like you, who are striving for success, are forced to face each and every day. How people overcome these obstacles depends on their personal situation, however, using a bit of creativity, employing hard work, and maintaining your all important determination toward achieving your goals will also contribute to your long-term success.

··

An obstacle is only an obstacle if you allow it to be one. Based on your knowledge, skills, education, and drive, use the resources you have available to continuously find ways around the obstacles you're confronted with. Thus what may seem like an obstacle may not in fact be one once you put your mind to overcoming it.

··

This list of potential obstacles will help you to start thinking about what may be holding you back and offers some possible solutions. However, it is a necessarily broad look at these obstacles. Some problems may require a more in-depth analysis to understand and solve. While this list doesn't address every problem or offer every possible solution, it does demonstrate the type of problem-solving attitude that will help you overcome your own problems to success.

Some of the most common (often perceived) obstacles that can keep people, just like you, from achieving their goals include:

1. *Lack of Money*

   There's a common misconception that to make money, you need to spend money. Thus, if you don't have money to begin with, your chances of making more money are greatly reduced. This simply isn't the case most of the time. If you're looking to start your own business, for example, there are many ways of raising start-up capital through borrowing money from family members, a financial institution, or venture capitalists. If your business idea is a good one and your business plan is strong, finding the money to launch your business can be achieved.

   Likewise, to meet your financial or personal goals, if you need money in addition to what your job currently pays you, there are plenty of opportunities available to you. For example, if you're looking to pay off your credit card debt in three years, you could work with a certified financial planner or accountant to analyze your ongoing spending habits, help you reduce your living expenses, and/or improve the return on your investments. You could also use time management techniques to help free up some of your time so that you can take on overtime work or a second job, if necessary, to improve your income immediately.

Other longer-term options might be to return to school or take courses that will improve your skill set, allowing you to get promoted to a higher paying job or pursue other more lucrative career opportunities.

Excessive spending and living beyond your means can be very tempting, especially using credit cards; however, with careful financial planning and long-term career planning, you can discover ways of better managing your finances and stretching the dollars you earn.

2. *Personality*

Your personality plays a major role in how people perceive you and in the reputation you create for yourself over time. If you maintain an outgoing and friendly personality and become known as someone who is trustworthy, hard-working, dedicated to their job, and who goes out of his or her way to help others, your career will benefit dramatically. If people truly like and respect you, they'll go out of their way to help you and to want to work with you. As a result, more career advancement opportunities will be presented to you.

If, however, you develop a reputation for being difficult to deal with, or for having a bad attitude, this will negatively impact your career. Having a poor reputation will ruin career advancement opportunities, and could easily negatively impact employee evaluations, new job interviews, and opportunities to earn promotions or raises.

Think carefully about the image and personality you convey now. Are you genuinely friendly and outgoing? What do you think people say about you behind your back? What do your superiors at work think of you? What could you change about your personality to improve how others perceive you?

There are many personality traits that can hinder a person's success. By answering the questions in Chapter 1, you may have discovered some habits or aspects of your personality that you or others consider negative. Many negative habits or personality traits can be overcome simply by recognizing them and making an effort to correct them.

For example, you may tend to be self-centered or unsympathetic. You may have trouble controlling your anger. You may lack confidence and the ability to assert yourself, whether at work or in your personal life. Or you may have trouble managing stress. Any of these personality traits will have an impact on your ability to achieve your goals.

It is beyond the scope of this book to address each potential personality issue. It is important for you to honestly assess your personality, and ask others for their honest assessment. If the problem you are facing seems too difficult to correct simply through awareness and the desire to change, you can consider seeking counseling. Traditional therapy is one option, but you can also explore special workshops designed to address particular problems such as stress reduction, anger management, or assertiveness training.

3. *Lack of Motivation and Drive*

Developing a set of ambitious goals is one thing, but having the drive, motivation, and/or determination to follow through and work toward making your goals a reality is entirely different. Some people spend their professional lives, day after day, being totally miserable, yet they're unwilling or unmotivated to do something to bring about a positive change. These people refuse to take their professional destiny into their own hands and control it.

Likewise, some people start off a new job or new project extremely motivated, but quickly lose focus on what they're trying to accomplish, or they encounter some unforeseen obstacle and wind up losing their motivation to succeed.

Different things motivate different people. As you begin setting personal and professional goals for yourself, it's important to determine what your true motivation is for developing each goal, and then figure out what it will take to keep you motivated on a day-to-day basis, no matter what challenges you face.

If you're doing something you have a passion for, chances are your passion will naturally motivate you. Likewise, if as you begin to work toward achieving your short-term and long-term goals, you see steady progress, this progress will also go a long way toward keeping you highly motivated.

Knowing what motivates you and never losing sight of what you're trying to accomplish will definitely help you stick to your action plans and stay motivated. Perhaps you'll also be motivated by receiving the praise or support of those around you, whether it be from your superiors at work, your coworkers, your friends, or your family members.

To help you discover some of the things that motivate you, answer these questions:

Based on your life right now, what motivates you to wake up each morning and have a positive outlook on your personal and professional life? _____

_____

_____

_____

If your life isn't going as well as you'd like it to right now, what could motivate you to make positive changes?

_____

_____

_____

_____

In your personal and professional life, what really excites you?

_____

_____

_____

_____

4. *Lack of Education*

For some people, a lack of skills, education, or experience prevents them from moving their career forward. If one of your professional goals is to become a senior vice president at your company, but to reach this level of success you will be required to earn an MBA, for example, then going back to school to pursue this degree is a necessary steppingstone to achieving the success you're ultimately looking to achieve.

If you're looking to earn a pay raise but maintain your current position, learning one or more new skills so you can enhance your value to your employer and take on additional responsibilities will most certainly help you achieve this goal, plus make you more marketable in the future.

Even if you must work full-time in order to earn a living, pay your bills, and support your family, chances are, if you made the temporary sacrifice of giving up your evenings and weekends to return to school or take classes on a part-time basis (or through a distance learning program, for example), you would eventually obtain the additional education you need to move your career forward or be able to change your career all together.

5. *Poor Organization and Time Management Skills*

There are many reasons why people who are qualified to fill the job they're hired for do not meet the responsibilities of their job. Having poor time management or organizational skills is one such reason. It can have a strong negative impact on your career as well as your personal life. After all, if you find yourself working 12 to 14 hour work days, simply because you're unable to complete your work-related responsibilities in a traditional eight hour work day, your personal life will suffer.

How much time in a typical day do you spend doing unimportant tasks? Do you find yourself unable to stay focused on important tasks at hand? Are you always running late for appointments or missing deadlines? If you could free up one, two, or even three hours per day, how would you spend that time? Would you more easily be able to achieve your long-term personal or professional goals if you had more free time? How would your attitude toward life in general change if you had more quality time to spend with your friends and family?

Simply by learning how to better organize your life and improve the way you manage your time, you could easily wind up being able to accomplish more and reduce the stress in your life. Chapter 6 of this book is dedicated to helping you master time-management and organizational skills that will improve your personal and professional life.

If every moment that you're awake is dedicated to playing "catch up" at work or in your personal life, finding time to get ahead will be extremely difficult. Learning how to better manage your time and adopt a more organized approach to the way you do things requires only a little bit of new knowledge; it also requires a commitment on your part to adopt that new knowledge and change your habits.

Learning to effectively use a daily planner, for example, is one way to better plan your time and organize your life. However, if you purchase the planner, but don't have the discipline to use it consistently, the positive impact this potentially powerful time management tool could have on your life will be minimal at best.

As you learn new time management skills and discover new tools for better managing your time or organizing your life, it's critical that you adopt the proper attitude and discipline to use this knowledge and the tools at your disposal.

Lack of time and organization can be a major obstacle in your personal or professional life, but they don't have to be!

6. *Lack of Focus Relating to Your Objectives and Goals*
Many people go through their daily routine at work or at home and never really think about their long-term goals or objectives. As a result, they lose focus on where they're going or what goals they're hoping to achieve. Without developing a focus and knowing exactly what you're trying to accomplish, and why, your ability to accomplish anything significant is greatly diminished.

Once you have your goals established and you develop your action plan(s), don't allow yourself to become side-tracked or lose focus. This too will take dedication, motivation, and discipline, but the results will be well worthwhile.

To stay focused, continuously ask yourself questions such as:

- What is the ultimate outcome you're trying to achieve? How you go about achieving an outcome is far less important than actually achieving it. It will often become necessary to modify your action plan when trying to achieve a goal. As the familiar saying goes, "Always keep your eye on the prize!"
- What is the purpose behind the goal toward which you're working?
- What actions need to be taken in order to achieve your objectives?

7. *Feeling Trapped in a Dead-End Job*
Okay, so you've made a few bad career decisions and you've found yourself in a job that has no future potential. You've mastered the job you're in, it offers little or no ongoing challenge, and there's nothing more you can learn. Yet, your employer offers no additional training, no career advancement potential, and no opportunity to move higher within

the company. You know, without a doubt, that what you're doing each day on the job right now is the same exact thing you'll be doing in six months, one year, or even five years from now.

Instead of wasting more of your professional life in a frustrating job, don't allow the bad career decisions you've made be an ongoing obstacle. Based on everything you've learned about yourself professionally from your answers to the questions in the previous chapters, begin updating your resume and exploring other career opportunities in a work environment in which you will better prosper.

As you evaluate new job opportunities, make sure the position offers advancement opportunities within the company and that you'll be able to take advantage of job training, if necessary, to pursue career advancement once you've proven yourself in the new job you're hired to fill.

Make sure the new job opportunities you explore will be steppingstones in your career path that will ultimately allow you to reach your long-term career objectives and goals, whatever they might be. Never settle for a dead-end job or be too lazy to do the research necessary or too afraid to ask the appropriate questions in order to ensure that the next career move you make won't become a dead-end job. Knowing what you're looking for, asking questions, and doing research are the easiest and most foolproof ways to ensure that the job you're being offered isn't being misrepresented.

All too often, applicants apply for what sounds like the ideal job, only to have their expectations shattered when they discover that how the job was advertised was misleading or misrepresented. No matter how well a job opening is described, it's your responsibility as the applicant to ask specific questions to avoid misunderstandings and to insure that the job you accept is the one you actually want and for which you are qualified.

When applying for a job, you have several opportunities to learn as much as you can about the expectations of the employer and the actual responsibilities of the position. If you're responding to a "help wanted" ad, one of the first things to ask a potential employer is for a detailed job description.

Most of the time, companies that misrepresent job openings do so unintentionally. When discussing a job opportunity with a potential employer, ask specifically what the responsibilities of the job are. If the employer uses descriptive phrases like, "work in a low stress environment" or "flexible work hours," have them define exactly what is meant. Often, how the employer defines terms in their job descriptions is different from how the applicant defines them. This is what leads to misunderstandings. Ask questions such as, "If I were to accept this job, what would you expect me to accomplish in the first three months and in the first year?" and "What kind of a person is successful in this organization? What do they do, and what are they like?" As you ask these questions, push the employer to provide complete answers about what will be expected of you.

Prior to an interview, prepare a list of at least five questions that you can ask to help you better understand the position for which you're applying. Before accepting a job offer, ask to speak with someone at the company who will be your colleague. As you interact with potential co-workers, ask yourself if you would enjoy working with these people on a daily basis.

If the employer states that you'll eventually be able to move up within the company, ask about training opportunities, how employees are evaluated, and how soon you could be considered for a promotion.

Plenty of great jobs are available, but to find the position that's right for you it's your responsibility to ask questions about the company, before accepting a job offer. If you know what you're getting into, you can easily avoid unwanted surprises and avoid dead-end and/or boring jobs.

8. *You Have Too Many Family-Oriented Responsibilities*

    Perhaps you're a parent of a newborn child, you already have kids you're trying to raise to the best of your abilities, you're involved in a serious relationship (but not married), or you have aging parents you are responsible for supporting. For many people, family responsibilities and the responsibilities of a serious relationship are a lot to juggle when they're trying to jump-start or maintain a successful career.

    When your decisions impact those you care about and who live with you (or whom you support), the ramifications of your decisions will be much greater than if you simply had your career objectives to consider.

    For example, if you're offered a job in another city that will require you to relocate, moving your entire family is a tremendous decision. While you could potentially earn a higher salary by accepting the job offer, seriously consider the impact the move will have on your spouse and children, as well as your own personal life. Will your spouse have to give up his or her career? Will your children be forced to leave their school and friends? What about your overall happiness and the happiness of those close to you?

    Having a family can at times prevent you from making changes that could be beneficial to your career. In these cases, you'll need to determine ways you can move your career forward without it having a negative impact on those close to you.

    There will be times, however, when making a short-term sacrifice will lead to greater long-term success. For example, if you work full-time, you might choose to attend classes in the evenings and on weekends in order to earn a degree that will ultimately allow you to earn more money. While you're actually attending school, you'll have much less time to spend with loved ones; however, once you graduate, your earning potential will increase and you'll again have time to spend with family and friends.

It's important that your family supports you in significant career-related decisions. For example, if you decide to return to school they will need to understand that for months or maybe years, your quality time with them may be dramatically reduced. This should be a decision with which everyone involved is comfortable.

Consider how your career success will benefit your family. For example, will the increased earning potential that will result from your degree allow you to achieve your family's goal of sending your children to college? Often decisions that benefit your career will also benefit those who are close to you and whom you support. Include your family in your decision-making. If you can include them in your plan for success, your ability to achieve your goals will be much greater than if you are met with resistance at every step.

As you embark on making your career-related goals a reality, never lose sight of your personal goals and how the decisions you make and the actions you take will impact the people you love. If your career-related goals and the goals of your family seem to be at complete odds and you and your loved ones cannot agree on a common set of goals, you might consider family counseling to come up with a working model for career success that allows you to meet your family obligations.

9. *Lack of Outside Support*

Are you one of those people who was supposed to follow in your father's footsteps, for example, and take over the family business, but instead you chose to follow a different career path? Do the people close to you for some reason not support the career path you've chosen? Are you working toward goals that the people you love don't agree with, understand, or support?

One of the greatest resources you can have as you set out to achieve your goals and dreams is having the support and encouragement of those you love. Having someone who will comfort you after a particularly difficult day and make you want to achieve success in everything you do is incredibly valuable.

As early in your life as possible, develop a strong support system for yourself. Your support system might include your parents, a spouse, relatives, close friends, or coworkers. These are people you can trust and with whom you can share your experiences, thoughts, fears, frustrations, and ideas. The people on your support team should be willing to provide you with love and encouragement as you face obstacles and pursue your goals. These people should offer you guidance and support when it's most needed.

One of the reasons why recovery programs like Alcoholics Anonymous work is because the people who are trying to become sober are given a support system to help them succeed. In your personal and professional life, the drive to succeed must come from within, but the ongoing encouragement and support you'll need should come from those close to you.

If you're able to develop a close-knit support group, you'll soon believe that anything is possible, because the people you choose to associate with will believe in you and help you maintain the motivation to succeed in whatever it is you set out to do. Try to surround yourself with positive and supportive people you respect and admire, and if possible, who are role models for you.

Not having a support system in place will not only make your quest for success a lonely one but will also put you at a significant disadvantage. Sure, it's possible to succeed without people cheering you on along the way, but the challenges will seem greater.

10. *You're Too Overwhelmed and Confused about Your Life and Career*
Unless you know exactly what it is you're trying to achieve, why you're doing what you're doing, and have an action

plan in place, accomplishing anything significant will be difficult because you will have little focus and direction, plus no deadlines to meet or specific objectives to accomplish.

Trying to accomplish too much, too fast is counterproductive, just as not knowing what you're trying to accomplish will make your life less focused. Simply by thinking about and answering the questions posed to you in this book, you'll be forced to focus on your goals and dreams and devise plans for making them a reality. Answering the questions in this book is step one. The next step relies on your own drive, creativity, and initiative.

11. *Religious Beliefs*

Just as you can encounter conflicts between your career and personal life, you might encounter conflicts with your spiritual beliefs. No matter what your religious beliefs are, it is important to adhere to those values, morals, and lessons that your faith has taught you. You should make time to fulfill your spiritual needs to the degree that they are important to you.

If you have questions about how your religious or spiritual beliefs can or should be incorporated into your personal and/or professional life, seek out the guidance of a religious leader, such as a priest, minister, or rabbi.

Your spiritual beliefs can be a tremendous source of motivation, hope, and internal strength, so it is important to achieve a balance and discover how to use your faith to help you achieve success rather than living with a spiritual conflict.

12. *Fear of Failure*

Someone who has failed at something in the past might be haunted by that experience for months or even years. This can easily cause insecurity and self-doubt which are ingredients for failure—not success. In order to get past a negative experience, consider what you have learned from the mistake or how you have grown from facing this difficulty. The same is true of overcoming a fear of failure. Consider that even if you fail at whatever it is you would like to try, you will learn and grow from the experience. Determine how you can grow from any failure and then focus on the future as opposed to dwelling on the past.

Everyone makes mistakes in his or her life. Those who learn from their mistakes and determine ways never to repeat them are the ones who most easily move forward in their lives and become the most successful.

13. *There's Too Much Stress in Your Life*

Let's face it: We're living in a fast-paced, highly competitive world where stress is a major part of our everyday lives. Those who learn how to cope with their stress and deal with it are at a significant advantage over people who dwell in stressful situations and take their stress home with them from work (or take their stress from home to work).

One of the best ways of eliminating or greatly reducing stress in your life is to understand what causes it and to find ways of coping with or getting rid of it. Living with ongoing stress isn't healthy from a mental or physical standpoint. Obviously, some jobs are incredibly stressful. That's the nature of the work. However, learning how to leave that stress at work and be relaxed when you come home at the end of the day, for example, is critical.

If you find yourself in a constantly stressful environment or living with stress on a daily basis that becomes too intense to deal with, consider participating in a stress management course offered at many hospitals. You can also seek the guidance of a doctor or trained medical professional, or take active steps in your life to reduce or eliminate the stress yourself.

For some, simply spending a short amount of time every day (or several times a week) pampering themselves is a way of relieving stress. Receiving a massage, taking a hot bath, going for a walk in the park, burning aromatherapy candles, doing yoga/meditation, taking a well-deserved vacation, or going to the gym after work are all excellent stress relievers.

Ask yourself:

In your life right now, what type(s) of stress do you experience on an ongoing basis?

_____

_____

_____

What causes your stress?

_____

_____

_____

When do you feel the most stressed?

_____

_____

_____

_____

What do you enjoy doing that helps you to relieve your stress?

_____

_____

_____

_____

What negative impact does stress have on you mentally and physically?

_____

_____

_____

_____

Can the things in your life that cause high levels of stress be eliminated from your life? If so, how?

_____

_____

_____

How much time do you spend each day or week taking steps to relieve your stress? Specifically, what steps do you take?

_____

_____

_____

What can be done, starting immediately, to give you additional time in your schedule to reduce the stress with which you currently deal?

_____

_____

_____

If you were to take an extra hour per day (or every other day) to pamper yourself and become more relaxed, how much more productive could you become during the rest of your day? How would this additional productivity benefit you?

_____

_____

_____

DEVELOPING YOUR PERSONAL AND PROFESSIONAL SKILL SET

One of the things that make you special and unique is your personal and professional skill set. This skill set is established in part through formal education, but expands with life experience and with the additional formal or informal training you receive through-out your life.

In today's business world, when an employer advertises a job opening, a listing of core requirements, such as education, a pre-determined amount of work experience, and a basic list of skills will be conveyed. It's basically assumed that everyone who applies for the job opening will meet those core requirements. What will ulti-mately determine if you get hired, however, will be your personali-ty and your unique skill set.

Employers will want to know how your skill set will make you a more valuable employee and how your skills can be used to best meet the responsibilities of the job. Being able to clearly define your skills and showcase them in qualitative and quantitative terms to a potential employer is an absolute must.

Some core skills are taught in school. Others, however, you can teach yourself or obtain through outside training. Depending on the type of work you do and the career path you choose to follow, the skills that will be in demand by employers will vary greatly.

The following are some of the more marketable skills that can be beneficial to almost anyone, pursuing any type of work:

- **Computer Skills**
- **Additional Languages (Being Bilingual or Multilingual)**
- **People-Management Skills**
- **Organizational Skills**
- **Speed-Reading Skills**
- **Time-Management Skills**
- **Verbal Communication (Public Speaking) Skills**
- **Written Communication Skills**

If you don't already have the desired skills, many of them can be obtained by:

- Listening to instructional audiotapes or CDs
- Participating in online distance learning programs
- Participating in on-the-job training
- Participating in traditional correspondence courses
- Reading self-help or instructional books
- Taking adult education classes
- Taking night classes at a college or university
- Taking professional development seminars
- Watching instructional videotapes

Many of these skills are relatively easy to learn, but can dramatically increase your earning potential, marketability as a job applicant, and your ability to receive promotions as an employee.

OBTAINING ADDITIONAL EDUCATION

Depending on the skills you want to acquire, you may determine that you want to return to school and pursue an additional degree or professional license. Before deciding to make this significant time and financial investment, consider what you're trying to accomplish. Ask yourself:

What specific knowledge or training are you looking to obtain?

_____

_____

How is this knowledge or education best obtained? What options are available? _____

_____

How will you benefit from obtaining this additional knowledge or education? _____

_____

How will your earning potential change as a result of this education or training? _____

_____

_____

What will be the time commitment involved? _____

_____

What type of financial investment is required? _____

_____

How will you pay for this education or training? Will your employer pay? Student loan? Scholarship? Savings? _____

_____

What's the downside to pursuing the education or training?

_____

How will obtaining the additional education or training impact your family and loved ones?

_____

_____

How will it impact your current job and ability to meet your current professional obligations and commitments? _____

_____

_____

As someone looking to continuously move his or her career forward and enhance their personal and professional skill set, making the decision to acquire new knowledge and skills should be an easy one. Pinpointing the skills or knowledge you want to acquire should be based (at least from a professional standpoint) on what will help you move your career to the next level. How you decide to pursue this knowledge or education will be based on your financial situation and available time.

Learning any new skill will require a time commitment on your part. Once you have the new skill, it will take additional time and practice to perfect or master it. After you have obtained the new skill or knowledge, you'll be able to put it to use, which is when you'll reap the rewards.

Just as professional skills help make you more marketable and valuable to an employer, developing your personal skill set can also make you a more well-rounded individual. Pursuing new hobbies, for example, will help you get the most out of some of your free time and possibly help you learn new skills.

There are also ways of combining the need to learn or master professional skills with personal interests. For example, if you're beginning to learn how to use computers, instead of starting off by trying to figure out difficult business programs and complex software, try learning to play a computer game you'll actually enjoy. Once you're comfortable learning to use the keyboard, mouse, and basic commands to play the game, for example, learning to use the same computer for business purposes will be much easier.

Just because you need to acquire specific skills for work, it does not mean learning those skills needs to be a boring or tedious process. If you need to do a lot of reading in your line of work, for example, consider taking a speed-reading course. During the course, as you learn the skills necessary, choose books you'd like to read for pleasure, so the content is enjoyable. Not only will acquiring the speed reading skills help you get through more work-related material faster and give you much greater retention, you'll have more time to read for pleasure and do other things you enjoy.

Part of becoming successful and learning how to coach yourself to success involves tapping your own creativity and thinking in new and innovative ways. In the next chapter, you'll discover more about how to pinpoint your strengths and showcase them, while understanding your weaknesses and learning how to overcome or compensate for them.

SUCCESS STORY:
Erica Overcomes an Obstacle

ERICA WAS A senior in college and still unsure of her plans for after graduation. She was a psychology major with a minor in computer science. She really wanted to become a programmer but thought that not having a computer science degree or any relevant "real world" experience would be too great of an obstacle.

When she interviewed for a few programmer positions she found that her feeling was grounded in reality. She learned that her lack of experience was a real obstacle preventing her from achieving her goal. However, Erica knew that this was the career she wanted; she knew that she was a good programmer and that she really loved the work. This helped motivate Erica to look for a work-around solution. She started looking for a related position that might serve as an entry into the field so that she could work her way toward her goal of becoming a programmer.

Through her job search she learned of and applied for a part-time position at an Internet company as a content editor. She was offered the job based on her writing skills that she had acquired as a psychology major. In her interview she expressed her long-term goal of working with the technical department, and the company let her know they would keep her interest in mind. Erica started at the company while she was in the final semester of her senior year, and as graduation approached she again expressed her interest in gaining a full-time position in the technology department.

Erica also focused on her work as a content editor and made a good impression on her supervisor. As a result, her supervisor, who knew of Erica's long-term goal, made sure to mention Erica's interest and talent to his contacts in technology department. Then, one day, a manager from the technology department approached Erica to let her know that a position was opening up in the technology department. She had already proven herself to be a loyal and valuable employee and had earned an in-house recommendation from her supervisor in the editorial department, so she was one-step ahead of her competition. Erica and the technology manager discussed Erica's abilities as a programmer and she was offered the position.

Erica now works as a programmer for a company that she loves. She is learning so much on the job that her lack of a computer science degree hasn't proved to be the obstacle she thought it might be.

C H A P T E R 4

analyzing your strengths and identifying your weaknesses

NO MATTER WHAT you set out to do, to be successful at it, you'll need to understand what your personal strengths are and discover innovative ways of using those strengths to your utmost advantage. At the same time, you should know where your weaknesses lie and discover ways to overcome them.

Understanding your strengths and identifying your weaknesses is a process of self-discovery. In earlier chapters, you answered a lot of questions pertaining to areas of your life, such as what you like to do, what skills you have, and what you do particularly well. Now it's time to focus in on those answers to summarize yourself, for yourself.

Let's start by analyzing the positives. If you're still in school (or a recent graduate) and you're looking to define a career path for yourself, defining your work-related strengths might seem a little difficult since you probably have minimal real-world work experience to draw upon. If you're in this situation, or if you're someone looking to change the focus of your career path, think about the work experience you do have and your education as you summarize your strengths. You should also think about activities you participate in—sports, volunteering, religious, or others—through which you may have gained valuable experience and developed your talents.

In terms of your career, a strength can be something you're particularly good at (and hopefully enjoy doing). Having a specialized skill and/or extensive knowledge of a topic (making you an expert in your field) are also strengths. Just about anything you can use on the job in order to help you meet the responsibilities of your position and excel can and should be considered a strength.

Everyone has a unique set of strengths. It's this combination of strengths that, when it comes to your career, will make you marketable to employers. The following is a brief list of strengths you may or may not possess. Place a check-mark next to those strengths you believe you posses, then in the blank spaces provided, add to this list by describing any other strengths you possess.

Keep in mind, the strengths you list do not have to relate directly to your career or job. A strength might be a skill you have, but that you don't actually use on the job. Or, it might be an aspect of your personality, background, religious beliefs, spirituality, education, or way of living that makes you a better overall person.

In defining your strengths, once again it's important to be totally honest with yourself. Hopefully, as a result of reading this chapter, not only will you define the strengths you currently posses, you'll also identify strengths you want to posses in the future, and develop a plan for achieving those strengths.

The following is a list of strengths. This is by no means a complete list. It was compiled to give you some direction as you put together your own list of strengths.

Place a check mark next to each item on this list that applies to you:

_____ Accept and easily cope with change

_____ Computer literate

_____ Family oriented

_____ Good listener

_____ Open minded

_____ Outgoing personality

_____ Strong interpersonal skills

_____ Strong managerial skills

_____ Strong mathematical abilities

_____ Understanding of financial issues

_____ Strong organizational skills

_____ Strong public speaking skills

_____ Strong time management skills

_____ Strong written communication skills

_____ Well-spoken

_____ Care about the well-being of others

_____ Enjoy reading

_____ Strong support system in place (professionally and personally)

_____ Respect for authority

_____ Look at failure not as a bad thing, but as an educational experience

_____ Maintain an overall positive mental attitude

_____ Make friends easily

_____ Manage stress well (can leave work-related stresses at work, and personal-related stresses at home)

_____ Possess natural leadership abilities

_____ Stay informed of important issues relating to you and stay aware of current events

_____ Take direction well

_____ Take pride in your appearance

_____ Work well under pressure

_____ Creative in terms of your thinking and how you go about doing things

_____ Deadline oriented

_____ Good at multitasking and taking on several responsibilities or projects at once

_____ Honest and have excellent personal and professional morals, ethics, and values

_____ Motivated and passionate in whatever you do

_____ Not afraid to ask for help or ask questions of others when necessary

_____ Supportive of others

_____ Willing to try new things

_____ Motivated by money

_____ Motivated by a drive to achieve personal and/or professional goals

_____ Motivated by (fill in the blank) _____

What specific skills or strengths do you posses that can (or do) directly help you on the job or in the pursuit of your career? How do you utilize each of these skills? A specific strength or skill might be the ability to perform a task that's specifically related to your job, the possession of a professional degree or license you've earned, or the ability to expertly operate specific types of machinery, whether it be a high-end photocopy machine, computer, or forklift. Some strengths are general, while others are job or industry-specific.

Skill:_____ How Utilized: _____

Skill:_____ How Utilized: _____

Skill:_____ How Utilized: _____

Skill:_____ How Utilized: _____

Skill:_____ How Utilized: _____

Skill:_____ How Utilized: _____

Skill:_____ How Utilized: _____

Skill:_____ How Utilized: _____

Skill:_____ How Utilized: _____

Skill:_____ How Utilized: _____

Think about why, specifically, you're good at what you do. For example, if you're a good manager, what skills and strengths do you utilize that help you excel at your job? Being a good manager requires you to possess many skills and to be able to utilize them simultaneously. Five skills or strengths that might allow you to be a good manager include:

- Being able to work well with others
- Being deadline oriented
- Being a good listener
- Being well organized
- Being able to cope well with stress

If you're a salesperson, for example, some of your top skills and strengths might include:

- Being a good communicator
- Having a strong working knowledge of your product(s)
- Being able to transform rejection into sales
- Being highly motivated
- Having strong telephone (telemarketing) skills

Make sure you give yourself ample credit for everything you're good at and that you enjoy doing. Just because a specific strength comes easily to you or is a natural ability you've never sought training for, chances are it's still incredibly valuable. Something that may seem trivial to you may, in fact, be something an employer will perceive as useful and valuable.

Everyone is born with at least a few natural abilities. Some people are naturally skilled at writing, doing math, or thinking logically. Others have artistic or musical abilities, for example. As you pinpoint your strengths focus in on your natural abilities and learn how to utilize them to your utmost advantage. It may take some creativity on your part to find ways to make some of your natural abilities useful on the job. Just because something isn't obvious, don't think it's not possible.

Having trouble defining your own strengths? Gather a list of help wanted ads or job descriptions from employers for positions you're qualified to fill. You can obtain these from any major newspaper, industry trade publication, or from career-oriented websites. In the help wanted ads and job descriptions, employers will often list the basic skills they're looking for qualified applicants to possess. If you have the skills in demand, consider these things to be among your strengths.

Once you know exactly what you're strengths are, the next step is to define exactly what you need to accomplish to excel at your job or in order to achieve your personal or professional goals. Knowing what needs to get done and what abilities you have will allow you to create a realistic action plan that will ultimately drive you toward success. The next chapter of *Your Career: Coach Yourself to Success* focuses on creating an action plan for achieving each of your short-term and long-term goals, dreams, and objectives.

IDENTIFYING YOUR WEAKNESSES

Now, let's take a few moments to think about your weaknesses. For most people, it's difficult to confront their inadequacies, but by doing so you'll eventually be able to overcome them and enhance who you are.

Remember, nobody is perfect, knows everything, or is highly skilled at everything he or she does. As you think about your weaknesses, don't consider them to be negative aspects of your life—they don't have to be! Think of a weakness as knowledge you haven't yet acquired or a skill you haven't yet learned. People who are truly driven to success use their determination, ambition, and creativity to pinpoint their weaknesses and find ways to overcome them.

If you think of all your weaknesses in these terms, none of them (whether real or perceived) are permanent. In fact, once you identify what knowledge, skills, education, and experience you lack, you can immediately begin to remedy the situation, transforming your weaknesses into strengths.

As you overcome some of your weaknesses by obtaining additional knowledge through education, training, and experience, you'll quickly discover that you'll identify new areas of knowledge and different skills that you don't yet have. The pursuit of knowledge is a never-ending process. Thus, even if you've graduated from high school, college, and even graduate school, your quest for learning should never end.

How you go about obtaining new knowledge will vary. For example, you might not choose to attend classes at a formal college or university. But instead, to achieve all your dreams and objectives, you'll want to develop a mindset that makes you excited to always expand yourself as a person and want to learn new things.

Your continuing education may not come from the classroom. Instead, it may come from reading books, listening to self-help audio tapes, watching instructional videos, participating in online distance learning programs, taking advantage of on-the-job training offered by your employer, or participating in adult education programs offered in your community.

At this point in your life, it's important to determine what knowledge, skills, or areas of interest you are interested in pursuing. Next, pinpoint all of your options for obtaining the additional education and experience you require.

Looking at the list of strengths in the previous section of this chapter, next to which items did you skip placing a check mark? Are these skills or strengths you believe would be beneficial to you if you possessed them? How could obtaining a new skill or strength (from the list, for example) help you achieve your personal, professional, or financial goals or move your professional life forward?

In your day-to-day professional life, what tasks are you reluctant to do? What responsibilities do you wish you didn't have? While it may not be possible to eliminate these responsibilities or tasks from your job description (or delegate them to your subordinates), perhaps if you improved your skill set somehow, or furthered your professional education, the tasks you dislike or aren't good at will become easier and less time consuming.

By making something easier, chances are it'll be less stressful and take less time to complete. Thus, if you can accomplish the things you dislike in less time and with greater productivity, you'll have more time left over to pursue the things you enjoy doing or that are more important for achieving your goals or objectives. For example, as a salesperson you may be required to complete weekly travel and expense reports in order to get reimbursed for your expenses. You may hate spending time filling in the spreadsheet; however, if you learned the program, you might find the whole process would take half the time and would be much less frustrating.

Once you pinpoint what you're *not* good at, ask yourself why this is the case. Are you lacking knowledge, motivation, dedication, practice, or expertise? What can be done, starting today, to help you obtain whatever it is you're lacking? Ask yourself the following questions:

In your daily life at work, what are the tasks you least enjoy doing, but must spend doing? _____

_____

_____

_____

What skills do you posses that allow you to complete these tasks or responsibilities? _____

_____

_____

_____

What skills or tools are you lacking that could help you complete the aspects of your work that you don't enjoy in a more timely manner, without compromising your accuracy or attention to detail?

_____

_____

_____

Are you frustrated with the aspects of the work you don't enjoy because you're not good at doing them? What else might be the cause of your frustration? _____

_____

_____

_____

Based on the job description (created by your employer) for the position you currently hold, what skills do you currently lack that keep you from improving your productivity or accuracy?

_____

_____

_____

In the career path that you've outlined for yourself, what knowledge or skills do you currently lack that are keeping you from earning your next promotion, pay raise or from landing your dream job? What could you begin doing, starting immediately, to prepare yourself and gather the skills and knowledge you need to become qualified for the job you'd like to have as opposed to the one you have now?

_____

_____

_____

_____

What are the most common mistakes you make at work? When you make mistakes, what is the primary cause? Is it due to lack of focus or attention (carelessness), or do you lack specific knowledge or skills? What would happen to your career if you improved your productivity and accuracy? _____

_____

_____

_____

Do you find yourself being taken advantage of by fellow employees or superiors who pass their work along to you, giving you additional responsibilities, but you don't receive proper gratitude or credit for your extra effort? _____

_____

_____

_____

_____

Which of your personality traits impede you from achieving the on-the-job success you desire?_____

_____

_____

_____

_____

If you have a job that requires you read and analyze reports, and many of these reports are dozens, if not hundreds, of pages in length, chances are you could benefit by improving your reading speed and comprehension. By taking a speed-reading course, for example, you could potentially cut the number of hours spent reading reports, and at the same time, improve your comprehension and recollection of everything you read. Taking a speed-reading course requires a minimal time and financial commitment, and it's something you can do in your spare time. Yet, it's something that you could benefit dramatically from in your professional life.

Likewise, if you're required to analyze financial data for your company, becoming more proficient using the spreadsheet program used by your employer could save you considerable time and make your job easier. Mastering a software package (such as Lotus 1-2-3, for example) is something that can be done by taking classes, reading how-to books, or by watching instructional videos. Once again, obtaining this knowledge would require a relatively small time and financial commitment on your part, yet the ongoing benefit would be dramatic. There's a big difference between being able to fumble your way through using a software program because you're only mildly familiar with how to use it, and becoming proficient at utilizing all of a program's features to make your work easier.

By analyzing what your professional responsibilities are now (or will be in the future), you can focus on how to make yourself more qualified and skilled at completing the tasks expected of you. By working to improve your skill set and knowledge base, you'll be able to overcome your professional weaknesses and keep the forward momentum of your career going.

When you identify a weakness, resist the pitfall of being upset with yourself for having that weakness. This frustration can lead to accepting your (perceived) limitations rather than allowing you to recognize your weakness to motivate you to work harder to overcome the weakness, whether it's by obtaining additional education, putting in greater effort, or better focusing in on your objectives. Whether or not you're able to overcome most weaknesses will be based on the mindset you adopt on an ongoing basis.

Everyone who has achieved success in their life, whether it be personal, professional, and/or financial, has been forced to overcome obstacles and face challenges that might have at first seemed insurmountable. These people managed to achieve their success, because, among other things, they have:

- Learned how to control stress
- Discovered how to develop new skills or areas of knowledge required to keep their career moving forward
- Mastered ways of focusing on their strengths and utilizing them
- Learned from mistakes and constantly worked hard to ensure they're never repeated
- Discovered how to maximize their time
- Found ways to stay focused on personal, professional, or financial goals/objectives, without getting overwhelmed by insignificant details or issues

- Developed the skills needed to work well with others, including how to delegate responsibilities to others when appropriate
- Adopted a true passion for whatever it is they set out to do

One of the best ways to learn how to become successful is to study other people whom you respect and who have already achieved success. Chapter 9 focuses on choosing mentors and role models. Once you put together a list of potential role models or mentors, discover what makes them tick and do your best to duplicate their strategies for success.

Once you learn about the people you select as role models or mentors, through research and/or by spending time with them, you'll probably discover they don't possess magical powers or anything extraordinary that has allowed them to achieve success. Role models, no matter how famous and successful they are, are people, just like you. So, if you adopt the mindset that the people you want to ultimately be like (professionally and/or personally) are just like you, only more experienced or more educated, you will be able to find ways to follow in their footsteps.

Lack of self-esteem and fear are major (perceived) problems that hold people back and keep them from achieving success. No matter what others think about you, ultimately, it is you who must become comfortable and proud of yourself. It is you who must develop the internal drive to achieve success, and it is you who must create a plan for yourself in terms of how you'll go about achieving your goals and dreams.

Knowing that you're totally prepared, informed, educated, and skilled enough to face various situations in your personal and professional life will give you confidence. Experiencing success and developing real world experience will give you an additional confidence boost over time. Developing respect for yourself is something that you need to do. No matter what other people think about you, this can't control the level of self-respect you possess.

Everyone experiences fear. Some people learn how to face their fears and confront them head-on. Others discover other ways of dealing with their fears, while some people accept their fears and let them become debilitating factors in their lives. Which category you fall into when it comes to dealing with fear will have a tremendous impact on your ability to achieve success. Everyone is fearful at times of change, taking risks, or having to deal with situations they're uncomfortable with, among others.

If you're being paralyzed by fear, determine for yourself what is causing the fear and confront it head-on. What do you fear? What's the worst thing that could happen if your fear becomes reality? What steps can you take to ensure what you're fearful of doesn't ever happen? Are you afraid of a real or perceived threat? Are you afraid of physical harm, for example, because you're actually in danger? Or, are you simply afraid you're going to fail, so you don't bother even trying to succeed?

Take whatever time is necessary to focus on what you're afraid of and why, then determine what steps you need to take to overcome the fears that you believe are holding you back from achieving your true potential.

Before you can overcome your weaknesses, fears, and obstacles, the first step is to determine what exactly is holding you back. The questions posed to you earlier in this chapter should have helped you with this. The next step is to develop and adopt an action plan to ensure that whatever challenges you face won't hold you back. The next chapter will help you create and adopt action plans that work.

Be realistic; some challenges or obstacles simply can't be overcome. You'll probably find that some things are simply out of your control. In these situations, tap your creativity to find ways to work around the obstacles. Instead of allowing an obstacle or weakness to be a roadblock, at most, consider it a detour on the road to success and navigate your way around it. As you obtain more experience facing your obstacles and challenges head-on, you'll discover the mindset you ultimately adopt will play a tremendous role in your ability to actually achieve success.

If you truly believe what you're trying to accomplish is possible and within your means, you'll find ways to make things happen based on the resources available to you. If, however, you adopt the mindset that you can't achieve success, for whatever reason, your mind will be conditioned to accept this, and your chances of achieving your goals and dreams will be greatly reduced. Don't train yourself to accept roadblocks and defeat. Train yourself to think differently and learn how to overcome whatever blocks your path to success.

Part of this chapter dealt with something that few people enjoy thinking about—what makes them imperfect. Most people, and you're probably one of them, would prefer to avoid thinking about their fears, weaknesses, and the challenges they face. This is human nature. However, by confronting these shortcomings, whatever they may be, your chances of overcoming them become far greater. You also thought about your strengths; remember that these strengths can help you overcome your weaknesses.

Your Career: Coach Yourself to Success is all about learning who you are as a person, planning and then taking actions that will allow you to achieve your goals and dreams. Having a clear understanding of your strengths can help you market yourself and help you direct these strengths toward achieving your goals, including overcoming the weaknesses you've identified.

SUCCESS STORY:
Leila Overcomes a Weakness

LEILA WAS A music teacher at a K-8 private school. She was having trouble dealing with a coworker who was always sneaky and rude, and who constantly undermined Leila's authority in front of the children. Leila recognized that she did not manage confrontation well, and was not good at understanding people's motivations. Leila decided that she needed to find a way to work with the woman without the constant confrontations that marked their relationship, so she began researching methods of dealing with people. She discovered the Enneagram, which is a tool for learning about how people relate to each other. It delineates nine different personality types and describes the way each personality type perceives and deals with life. It helped Leila discover how people's habits of behavior impact the way that they deal with people, and affect how they make decisions.

Once Leila' realized her coworker's particular style and how she operated, she learned why her coworker was behaving in such a horrible way. When she learned not to take her coworker's behavior so personally, she was able to be compassionate but also could treat her in a way that meshed with her style. Although her coworker did not change, Leila was able to feel better about their exchanges, and she was also able to interact with her coworker more pleasantly.

Leila was also able to apply what she learned from studying the Enneagram to other professional and personal relationships. Once she was able to understand what was driving the actions and reactions of the people with whom she had to interact, she found herself working better with others. Of course learning about her own style and how she relates to others was also extremely helpful; Leila has found that the Enneagram continues to be a valuable tool in all of her relationships.

creating an action plan to achieve your goals

THE BIGGEST DIFFERENCE between those who have achieved success and those who have not is that the people who have gotten what they want out of life—whether personally or professionally—have taken action and have gotten things done for themselves.

These achievers don't rely on others or wait for opportunities to drop into their lap—they make things happen. Are you someone who goes after what you want with a drive and determination and who doesn't allow for failure? In the earlier chapters of this book, many of the questions posed were designed to help you clearly define your personal, professional, and financial goals, along with your dreams and long-term objectives.

As you have learned, before you can go about achieving goals, you must clearly define them so you know specifically toward what you're working. In addition, you need to understand what your true motivation is behind each goal you set. Ask yourself questions like:

- Why are you working toward a specific goal?
- Why do you want to achieve a specific outcome?
- What are the short-term and long-term objectives?
- What do you get out of achieving your goal?
- How will you benefit?
- What value do you place on the desired outcome of your goal?

You already know that the easiest way to make a goal, especially a long-term goal, achievable is to divide it up into a series of smaller, more achievable goals. As you evaluate your goals and divide them up into more manageable tasks or objectives, to achieve ultimate success, you will be developing an "Action Plan" for each short and long-term goal you set.

WHAT IS AN ACTION PLAN?

An action plan is your personalized road map that will lead you to success. It involves:

- Defining your objective(s)
- Understanding why you are pursing each objective (looking at the big picture)
- Setting up a timetable or schedule for achieving each objective
- Determining what steps need to be taken
- Actually taking the appropriate actions, on a day-to-day basis, to achieve your desired results or objectives

Small goals that don't require a lot of planning don't necessarily require a formal action plan. For larger, long-term goals, however, you'll want to create an action plan with as much preplanning and detail as possible, in order to help you understand step-by-step how you will meet your goal and stay focused on what you're trying to achieve.

As you become entrenched in the hustle and bustle of your daily routine, it's very easy to get caught up in unexpected emergencies. These situations often require your immediate attention, take up time, cause stress, and keep you from actually achieving what you need to do.

By combining your action plans with time management techniques, you'll be able to find more time in your day (or week) to deal with the emergencies, but at the same time, take the necessary actions that will lead you closer to achieving your goals.

When it comes to developing an action plan for achieving an important or long-term goal, you'll probably want to put your action plans in writing. To do this, you can use a pad of paper; a scheduling/time management or project management program on a computer; or a traditional daily planner or scheduler (such as one from Day-Timers or Day-Runner).

··

You can also use the scheduling/time management features of a personal digital assistant, such as the PalmPilot V (www.palm.com) to assist you in keeping your action plans organized and readily accessible. Time management tools are described in greater detail within Chapter 6.

··

Defining Your Action Plans

As you already know, the first step in creating an action plan is to clearly define your objective or goal. You also want to understand why you're trying to achieve the goal. Each time you create an action plan, you'll want to answer, in writing (or at least think about), the following questions:

Action Plan Worksheet

Define your goal: _____

_____

_____

_____

Describe (in detail) what you desire the outcome to be. (What is the desired result?): _____

_____

_____

_____

Why are you trying to achieve this desired outcome? _____

_____

_____

_____

What is the overall deadline or timetable for accomplishing the desired result or outcome? (Be sure to list a specific time of day, day of the week, and/or date. If this is a long-term goal, you might set a one-year, three-year, or five-year deadline, for example.)

_____

_____

_____

What are the specific steps you need to take to achieve the desired outcome? (Your specific goal may require only three steps or as many as ten or fifteen steps to achieve.) Be sure to break up monumental tasks into smaller, more achievable tasks that will help lead toward your desired outcome.

Step #1: _____

Step #2: _____

Step #3: _____

Step #4: _____

Taking into account your daily, weekly, and/or monthly schedule and responsibilities, how long do you anticipate it will take to accomplish each of the above mentioned tasks?

Step #1—Anticipated Time/Date to Accomplish: _____

Step #2—Anticipated Time/Date to Accomplish: _____

Step #3—Anticipated Time/Date to Accomplish: _____

Step #4—Anticipated Time/Date to Accomplish: _____

Step #5—Anticipated Time/Date to Accomplish: _____

Think about the importance of each step that needs to be accomplished to achieve your desired outcome or objective. Set priority levels for each step, placing the most important steps first. It may be helpful to rank each step using numbers between one and three (with the number one item being the most critical). In some cases one step must be completed before another (sometimes more important) step can be taken. You'll need to factor this into your prioritizing.

- #1 Priority—Something that must be accomplished immediately. Something listed in this category is extremely critical and time sensitive.
- #2 Mildly Important—These are things that need to be accomplished in order to achieve your goal, but there's no immediate urgency involved, and the order in which you accomplish these #2 ranked tasks isn't important.

- #3 Less-Important—To accomplish just about anything, chances are they'll be some busy work involved. While these items need to be accomplished at some point, there's no need to focus on items ranked at this level of importance until your more important items are dealt with appropriately.

If your action plan has many steps with varying levels of importance, you might prioritize them using numbers followed by letters. For example, one item may be ranked 1-A, while something that's equally as important, but that can't be accomplished until the 1-A item is complete, might be ranked 1-B.

By setting priorities for what you need to accomplish, you'll eventually be able to implement effective time management techniques so that you're spending your most productive time of the day focusing on 1-A, 1-B, and 1-C items, instead of insignificant 3-A, 3-B, or 3-C items.

As you begin learning about your own work habits, you'll be able to determine what times of the day you are the most productive. For example, some people are morning people and are the most productive and can think the most clearly early in the day. Others thrive after lunch or in the later hours of the day. Once you determine what your most productive time is, focus on completing your #1 ranked items during that time. Save the least important tasks for times of the day when you aren't as sharp and when productivity isn't as critical.

Using this method of prioritizing the steps in your action plan, reposition each step accordingly, listing the #1 priority items first. Remember, your list may include any number of steps, but it's best to keep the number of steps to between three and ten. (If you have more than ten steps, maybe you need to create two goal or action plans.) Next, incorporate this information into your daily planner or scheduler so you allocate specific times to work on each step/objective.

If you know step one is a high priority and will take five hours to complete, for example, find a block of time in your schedule to dedicate toward achieving that step or task. You might need to allocate one hour per day for five days if a five-hour block isn't available based on your other responsibilities.

(Prioritized Steps for Your Action Plan)

Step #1: _____

Step #2: _____

Step #3: _____

Step #4: _____

What obstacles or roadblocks do you anticipate facing? How will you deal with these situations as they arise?

_____

_____

_____

_____

Implementing Your Action Plans

Based on the steps outlined this far, for each goal you should:

1. Know exactly what needs to get done
2. Understand why each task or step needs to get done
3. Know specifically what you're trying to accomplish (the desired outcome)
4. Schedule time to accomplish your objectives and incorporate this information into your daily schedule or planner

Once these four basic steps are complete, it's time to actually get off your butt and start making things happen. Begin by looking at your list of steps and choose the first 1-A item on it. Figure out what you need to do to accomplish each task or step and it's time for action.

As each item on your list gets accomplished, place a check mark next to it within your written action plan (or in your planner), indicating it's complete. Throughout the day, week, or month, your obvious goal is to place as many check marks on your list as possible. As you add check marks to your list, you'll easily be able to measure your accomplishments and progress. Based on the time you allocated for each task, you'll know what still needs to get done. Seeing actual progress will help to keep you motivated, especially if you're passionate about what you want the outcome to be.

There will be times, for whatever reason, that a particular item on your list can't be accomplished at a specific time. When this occurs, don't brush aside your list and forget about your objectives. Instead, move on to items on your list, no matter how insignificant they are, that can be accomplished in the time you have available. Taking even the smallest steps forward toward achieving your desired outcome is much better than making no progress at all.

If you're driving a car, for example, it takes more energy to get that car moving again (and bring it up to cruising speed) from a total stop than it takes to regain speed while the car is still in motion, even if it's moving slowly. Likewise, if you've created momentum in terms of achieving your goals, it's far easier to keep that momentum going if you don't take a break from working toward achieving your desired outcome. This is why it's important to always be working toward accomplishing your desired outcome, even by doing the most insignificant tasks.

There will definitely be times when you'll need to revisit an action plan and modify it to accommodate a specific change in your schedule or to overcome an unexpected challenge. As you begin to work on your action plan, you might also discover in midstream a better or more productive way of doing something. As new experience and knowledge is acquired, incorporate it into how you go about implementing your action plans.

Why Some People Fail to Complete Their Action Plans

Even with an action plan in place, there are reasons why people don't succeed. After all, an action plan is nothing more than a plan to succeed. Once the plan is established, it has to be carefully and faithfully implemented. If you're dedicated enough to define your goals and objectives and then create an action plan, beware of the common pitfalls that keep some people from successfully completing whatever it is that their action plan spells out. These common pitfalls include:

- The Fear of Failure—If you're afraid to fail and that fear keeps you from pursuing your goals, you're destined to fail. Once you determine you're being held back by your fear, whether it's a reasonable fear or not, it should be dealt with head-on and eliminated (or at least kept under control).
- You Don't Know What To Do First—Most people have many goals. When they start creating action plans for each of their goals, they quickly become overwhelmed by the magnitude of the tasks ahead and find themselves feeling discouraged. Choosing priorities and pursuing what's important first, then breaking up large goals into smaller ones will help eliminate the feeling of being overwhelmed. Defining your priorities and what's important to you (and why) will help you decide what do to first.
- You Feel Unworthy—Some people work incredibly hard to achieve their goals, only to find that once they achieve success, they feel it isn't deserved. A feeling of guilt sets in that results in a lack of motivation to pursue future goals and objectives. Instead of simply choosing random goals to pursue, select goals that have value to you, in which the outcome will be meaningful on a personal and/or professional level. If you work hard to achieve something that is important to you on a deeply personal or professional level, you'll certainly feel the successful outcome is deserved once you achieve it.
- Laziness—There's really no excuse for laziness. If you want to get anything done in life, you need to face the challenges head-on and pursue the results you desire. One way to overcome laziness is to prepare a carefully defined action plan and schedule, then develop a system of rewarding yourself for reaching pre-defined milestones.
- Procrastination—You know something is important, but you lack the motivation to work toward achieving your desired

result. Instead, you choose to do something that offers more instant gratification or pleasure, but that doesn't help you obtain whatever it is you're trying to accomplish. Because you lack the urgency to do anything, what's actually important winds up getting pushed back or delayed. By delaying important tasks, you'll ultimately be forced to work under much greater pressure to meet deadlines. While some people thrive under pressure, most people can eliminate the urge to procrastinate by discovering better ways to keep themselves motivated. Knowing what you're trying to achieve, what the desired result is, why the result is important to you personally, and putting a personal value on that result will help create a greater sense of urgency. Taking these actions should reduce your urge to procrastinate.

- Lack of Patience—Many people want instant gratification and aren't willing to be patient and take the necessary steps toward achieving success. This is probably one of the biggest reasons why people fail to achieve their desired results after defining their goals and creating the appropriate action plans. Anything that is truly important and has value isn't going to be achieved quickly. Long-terms goals, by definition, take time, planning and hard work to achieve. Developing the mind set that you'll need to work hard over an extended period of time to achieve a desired result is critical for success. Setting mini-goals and a reward system for reaching milestones as you pursue long-term goals will help you to experience gratification faster than if you had to wait until an entire long-term goal is achieved.

Simply understanding some of the major reasons why people ultimately fail at achieving their desired results should help you avoid putting yourself in these situations. By developing action plans that have contingency plans built in along with a carefully thought-out schedule will keep you focused and keep your forward momentum going as you pursue your goals and objectives.

A SAMPLE ACTION PLAN

Ed has been working as an assistant in the marketing department of his company for a year. He just had his first review and he learned that while he is a very valued employee his boss doesn't think he is ready for a promotion. One of the responsibilities that would come with a promotion is presenting new products at the annual sales meeting. Ed's boss doesn't think Ed has the public speaking skills necessary to be successful at this task. Ed, who recognizes that he not very outgoing, is determined to prove that he is capable of presenting at the sales meeting.

Ed decides that he will improve his chances of getting a promotion if he makes a good impression when he presents his research at an internal marketing department meeting in December. It's October now, so he has two months to achieve his goal. His friend in the department recommends that he take a public speaking course at the local community college.

Here is Ed's action plan:

Define your goal: *Develop the public speaking skills necessary to speak before a large audience.*

Describe (in detail) what you desire the outcome to be: *Win my boss's confidence in my abilities and earn a promotion in six months.*

Why are you trying to achieve this desired outcome? *I want to take on more responsibility in the department and be able to take on more creative work. I also want to increase my salary so I can afford to move into my own place.*

What is the overall deadline or timetable for accomplishing the goal/outcome? *There is an internal meeting in which the assistants present their research reports to the marketing managers in two months. I would like to present with confidence at that meeting.*

What are the specific steps you need to take to achieve the goal? Taking into account your daily, weekly, and/or monthly schedule and responsibilities, how long do you anticipate it will take to accomplish each of the above mentioned tasks?

1. Research the public speaking courses at local colleges and training schools. Time to complete: 2 hours of surfing the Internet and making calls.
2. Review the materials and select the best course for me. Time to complete: 2 hours.
3. Register for the course. Time to complete: half hour.
4. Attend the course. Time to complete: 2 hours a week for 6 weeks (if I do the community college course).
5. Complete research for presentation. Time to complete: 10 hours.
6. Prepare presentation. Time to complete: 2 hours.
7. Practice presenting research. Time to complete: 2 hours.
8. Present research at the meeting. Time to complete: 1 hour.

What obstacles or roadblocks do you anticipate facing? How will you deal with these situations when they arise? *My softball team practice is on Wednesday nights, and the community college course is on the same night. If this is the best course, I'll have to miss the first half of the season. John (team captain) will probably give me a hard time. I'll explain how important this promotion is to me.*

I think the class might be hard for me—I really hate public speaking. I'll focus on my goal and remind myself why it is important for me to learn this skill.

With all of this information in place, Ed can take each of the eight steps involved in improving his speaking skills and rearrange them in order of priority. In this example, the steps are chronological so what Ed needs to focus on is fitting each of the steps into his existing schedule.

He puts each step into his planner so that he is sure that he can accomplish his goal in time.

He prioritizes the eight steps as follows:

1. *Research courses.*
   To be completed: this evening (Monday, October 3), between 7p.m. and 9p.m.
2. *Read material and select best course.*
   To be completed: Thursday evening (October 6), between 8p.m. and 10p.m.
3. *Register for course.*
   To be completed: Friday morning (October 7)

4. *Attend course.*

To be completed: as scheduled through college, but I must select a course that I can start and complete by the end of November.

5. *Complete research for meeting.*

To be completed: first week in December—spend two hours each morning researching.

6. *Prepare presentation.*

To be completed: Monday morning (December 9).

7. *Practice presentation*

To be completed: Tuesday and Wednesday evening at home—1 hour each evening.

Note: Ask John to come over Wednesday night and listen to presentation.

8. *Present at meeting.*

To be completed: Thursday, December 12, 11 a.m.

As you become more skilled at developing action plans, you can combine steps to save you time. For example, you'll eventually be able to define the steps that need to be achieved, allocate time for the completion of each task, and incorporate these tasks into your schedule, in one or two steps. But when you are starting to use action plans it is a good idea to plan out each step in detail. It will help keep you motivated and will help you to see in clearly defined steps how you will achieve your goal.

CHOOSING YOUR PRIORITIES

Depending on what type of work you do, the #1-A important tasks you're required to accomplish will vary. Just as you set priorities for your work-related goals and objectives, you can easily do the same for your personal and financial goals. Ultimately, what you spend your time doing should be important and have significance to you. If you clutter your entire day doing boring and insignificant tasks, not only will you get little accomplished in terms of achieving your goals, chances are you'll also grow extremely frustrated with your daily life and routine.

Make sure that at least a portion of your day—everyday—is spent doing things on your list of priorities that are important to you and about which you're truly passionate. Finding time to do this involves planning and careful scheduling.

There will be times, unfortunately, where sacrifices will need to be made in order to achieve one set of priorities over another. Before making decisions, think about the possible ramifications, measure the potential negative and positives results, and then make intelligent decisions. For example, if you need to complete a work-related project on time, it might require you to stay late at work. By staying late, you may have to give up having dinner with your family or cancel social plans that were important to you. In this particular situation, you'll want to consider if working late is worth sacrificing your social plans. Sometimes, this will be an easy decision, but not always.

Suppose your child suddenly catches the flu and needs to stay home from school. You don't have time to find a baby-sitter and it's important that you be there for your child. In this situation, you may be forced to choose between important work-related responsibilities (and deadlines) and your personal responsibilities at home.

There are no pre-defined rules for setting your priorities. Each situation needs to be evaluated separately and the decisions you make need to be made based on the potential outcome(s) that will be a result of your actions. By preplanning, however, you should be able to identify potential conflicts and situations that may arise and then develop contingency plans in advance for dealing with these situations.

MEASURING YOUR PROGRESS

Obviously, the best way to measure and evaluate your progress is to accomplish everything listed in one or more of your action plans and then reap the benefits of what you've achieved. Some goals, however, will take days, weeks, months, or even years to achieve. In these situations, it's important to keep careful track of the progress you make as you accomplish each step in each of your action plans.

Two of the questions posed to you earlier in this chapter were,

"What obstacles or roadblocks do you anticipate facing?" and "How will you deal with these situations when they arise?" Anything that keeps you from working toward achieving your objectives or your desired outcome is a potential obstacle or roadblock. As you begin working toward achieving the items in your action plan, if you're not making satisfactory progress, chances are you haven't accurately answered these two questions and you haven't created proper contingency plans for dealing with unexpected situations, schedule conflicts or other situations that arise.

As you reach milestones while working toward achieving your desired outcome(s), document these successes. This can be done in your personal planner, in a diary or on a sheet of paper.

You might also choose to set up a mini-reward system for yourself. For example, if your personal goal is to lose 15 pounds in two months, each time you lose five pounds, you might consider rewarding yourself by buying an item of clothing. It might help keep you motivated and help you see your progress. This would also help you take the monumental task of losing 15 pounds and divide it up into a series of smaller goals, which are to lose five pounds at a time.

There are many things you can do to keep yourself focused and motivated. For example, if your action plan consists of ten items that need to be accomplished in a day in order to achieve a short-term goal, reward yourself for achieving progress throughout the day. Once you complete three of the items on your list, reward yourself with a ten- or fifteen-minute break, or spend a few minutes doing something you truly enjoy.

VISUALIZE YOUR SUCCESS

Whether you're a professional athlete, business professional, or someone looking to achieve virtually any goal, one way to lead yourself to success is to participate in some simple visualization exercises. Everyone knows how to daydream. A visualization exercise simply involves seeing your success in your mind before it happens. In your mind, work through how you'll go about achieving each step that's necessary toward achieving your objective. See yourself successfully doing and accomplishing each step.

If you're going to be doing a speech in front of 30 people, for example, in your mind, see yourself in front of those people and entertaining them as you speak. Visualize what you'll be wearing, what gestures you'll make, what key points you plan to make, and what the intensity of your voice will be. Do several complete "dress rehearsals" in your mind—always visualizing the best possible outcome.

After doing this, think about some of the things that might go wrong and visualize what steps you'll take in order to fix any problems as soon as they happen. For example, instead of entering a state of panic, imagine how you will deal with the overhead projector going dead during your speech. If someone asks a question you don't know the answer to, how will you respond without looking foolish?

When preparing to make a presentation or give a speech, nothing replaces the need to do actual rehearsals; however, you can supplement that rehearsal anytime and anyplace using visualization techniques.

Professional athletes use visualization techniques before a game to prepare themselves emotionally and psyche themselves up. Many business people use this technique to help them succeed in their daily lives and prepare for important meetings, for example. If you're responsible for writing a business proposal, in your mind picture what the proposal needs to say and how the document will look once it's complete. Picture yourself doing the necessary research and then writing the proposal without encountering writer's block.

Whatever it is that you need to do, use visualization to plan out the details, in advance and in your mind. This way, when the time comes for something to actually happen in real life, you'll experience almost a sense of déjà vu because your mind will already be programmed for success.

Throughout this chapter, the importance of careful preplanning and scheduling all aspects of your action plan were emphasized. In the next chapter, you'll discover useful time management techniques and learn about specific tools you can begin using immediately to help you get the most out of your day.

SUCCESS STORY:
Alvin Creates an Action Plan

ALVIN WORKED FOR 15 years as a pediatrician at a large HMO. He was well respected, well-liked, and very good at his job. He really cared about his colleagues, patients, and coworkers. He was a busy man, with two active children and a wife. Although his mentor was constantly asking him to get involved in various hospital committees, he always declined because he felt that he would not have time to do other activities outside of the hospital.

However, when the department announced that the Chief of Pediatrics was planning to retire in three years, Alvin decided that this would be a good time to learn about the administrative side of the hospital. He knew that the current Assistant Chief of Pediatrics would probably move up into the Chief's position and he thought that he might like to be in the role of the Assistant Chief. After his mentor suggested again that he work toward the position, Alvin decided to take some action. He volunteered for several committees, became an active member of these committees, and spoke with the retiring Chief to get a better idea of what new duties he would have to accept as the Assistant Chief. In addition, the position was also enticing because he enjoyed working with the incumbent Chief, and also knew that he would earn more money in this administrative position.

After he set his goal, he really put his plan into action. He proved to the rest of the department that he was capable of his new duties: he planned meetings, suggested and launched new hospital programs, organized the staff schedules, and proposed new organizational strategies. He also established a good rapport with the Physician in Chief of the hospital. Thus, he worked hard to establish a strong organizational presence both in the pediatric department and throughout the rest of the hospital. As a result, after three years, when it came time for the Chief of Pediatrics to retire, Alvin had established himself as a dynamic administrator, and the deciding body concluded that Alvin would be the right choice for the next Assistant Chief of Pediatrics.

developing time management and organizational skills

THERE ARE ONLY 24 hours in a day. That's 168 hours in a 7-day week. According to a study conducted by Day-Timers, Inc., men work an average of at least 50 hours per week, while women work more than 42 hours per week.

How do you spend your time? Do you find yourself always running behind, under stress, trying to meet deadlines, and never able to find time for yourself or to spend with your loved ones? Day-Timers found that 62% of American workers feel they are always or frequently rushed to do the things they have to do, and only 8% of American workers describe themselves as extremely happy with their lives.

It is within your power, using basic time management and organizational skills, to be among the relatively few American workers who aren't constantly rushed and who are truly happy in their personal and professional lives.

There are many reasons why American workers as a whole aren't happy with their professional lives. Some people find themselves stuck in dead-end jobs, mainly because they never took the time to plan out their career path and set professional goals for themselves. These same people have often never discovered how to utilize effective time management or organizational skills.

Earlier in this book, you learned how to set personal, professional, and financial goals for yourself. This is something that fewer than 33% of American workers ever bother to do. In this chapter, you'll discover ways of making the most out of your time. Thus, in addition to meeting the day-to-day responsibilities of your personal and professional life, you'll discover how to find time to pursue your goals and have time to experience activities you truly enjoy.

People who have achieved success have almost always mastered the ability to set goals and plan, plus they have learned to combine these skills with time management and organizational techniques.

Learning to become a more organized person and to better utilize your time will mean learning a new set of skills and incorporating them into your life on an ongoing basis. If you choose to begin using a time management tool, such as a personal planner, for example, you must use it daily and readjust your habits accordingly. Buying a personal planner and throwing it into a drawer of your desk and never looking at it won't help you better manage your time and become more organized.

Becoming more organized and better managing your time will take a conscious effort and commitment on your part. Like any new skill, mastering these new skills will take practice. If you're willing to commit yourself to learning and perfecting these new skills, you'll see remarkable changes in the amount of time you have available, plus you'll notice greatly reduced levels of stress in your life.

At first, adopting these new skills and tools into your life may seem like it takes up time, rather than saving you time. Consider this learning curve as an investment. Depending on your personal situation and what skills and tools you decide to incorporate into your daily life, it might take between one week and one month for you to begin realizing the incredible benefits of time management and being better organized.

WHAT IS TIME MANAGEMENT?

There are 24 hours in a day, during which time you must meet your personal and professional responsibilities as well as eat and sleep. For most people, it's very easy to simply run out of time in the day, especially if you have a particularly challenging job and need to juggle it with a personal and family obligations.

Time management involves carefully analyzing how you currently spend every minute of your day and then determining ways you can make better use of those minutes. This often includes eliminating many or all of the time wasters that each of us must contend with on a daily basis. It also involves learning to set priorities and better focus on tasks and obligations at hand, while not getting bogged down with irrelevant details or trying to take on too much as once.

Studies show that most highly productive managers have learned to take on only about three major tasks or priorities each day. By spending time focusing on only a few important tasks at once (plus lesser important obligations), it's easier to focus your attention and dedicate the time necessary to accomplish what needs to get done. The result of taking on only a few important tasks at once is that these people are able to accomplish more on a consistent basis, and maintain a more motivated attitude, because by the end of each day they can always measure their positive results.

If you've already completed the questionnaires included earlier in this book and have begun setting short-term and long-term goals for yourself, you've taken some of the most important steps toward coaching yourself to success. Now, you need to discover the best ways of utilizing every minute you have available to get the most out of your personal and professional life. That's what time management is all about!

Let's Talk Organization

One of the biggest reasons why people never achieve their goals and never seem to have time in their day to accomplish what they need or want to do, is because of a lack of organization.

In your life, you can physically organize your workspace (your office, desk, file cabinets, paperwork, electronic files, etc.) and your home to provide for a more relaxed and productive environment. You can also organize how you spend your time. Organization goes hand-in-hand with time management, goal setting, and proper planning.

Just about everyone is surrounded by clutter, including mail, paperwork, e-mails, phone messages, magazines, newspapers, industry publications, and bills. One of the best ways to become more organized and save time is to eliminate as much clutter in your life as possible. Without clutter, whether it's physical clutter in the form of piles of paper, or more abstract mental clutter, you'll be able more easily to focus your time and energies on what's important in your personal and professional life.

Time Management and Organizational Strategies

Step one in learning time management skills is to determine exactly how you currently spend your time. The best way to do this is to dedicate one week to creating an activity journal. Use a personal planner, scheduling software, or even a pad of paper, and begin writing down everything you do each day and how much time it takes. Write down everything! How much time do you spend each day preparing and eating breakfast, commuting to work, reading your mail (and e-mail), talking on the phone, performing work-related tasks, doing busy work, working out at the gym, watching television, cleaning, etc. How much time do you spend sleeping?

For a one-week period, write down everything you do and how long it takes. Once this is complete, review your activity log and determine all the ways you waste time each day. While at work, for example, how much time do you spend reading junk mail, dealing with interruptions, and sitting in on meetings where nothing gets accomplished?

ACTIVITY LOG WORKSHEET

Create one worksheet for each day of the week you choose to study in your personal and professional life. As you do this, determine what time(s) of the day you're the most productive and think the most clearly. This should ultimately be the time you spend doing your most important work. The following sample worksheet is broken down into half-hour intervals.

DATE: 10/4/00
DAY OF THE WEEK: Wednesday

TIME OF DAY	ACTIVITY
06:01 A.M.–06:30 A.M.:	*sleeping*
06:31 A.M.–07:00 A.M.:	*sleeping*
07:01 A.M.–07:30 A.M.:	*sleeping*
07:31 A.M.–08:00 A.M.:	*awake, shower, brush teeth, put on makeup*
08:01 A.M.–08:30 A.M.:	*dry hair, dress, walk to subway*
08:31 A.M.–09:00 A.M.:	*train to work—read article in "New Yorker"*
09:01 A.M.–09:30 A.M.:	*buy coffee and bagel, walk to work, eat breakfast, read e-mails, NYT online*
09:31 A.M.–10:00 A.M.:	*talked to Mark about plan for Columbus Day weekend*
10:01 A.M.–10:30 A.M.:	*did some research into competitors for the spring product line*
10:31 A.M.–11:00 A.M.:	*answered e-mail concerning new ad campaign*
11:01 A.M.–11:30 A.M.:	*got water, bathroom, read article Paul left on my chair*

11:31 A.M.–12:00 P.M.: *checked out cheap fares on travelocity.com, made some calls about B&Bs in VT*

12:01 P.M.–12:30 P.M.: *staff meeting*

12:31 P.M.–01:00 P.M.: *lunch with Cara, talked about some workflow problems in marketing dept.*

01:01 P.M.–01:30 P.M.: *lunch*

01:31 P.M.–02:00 P.M.: *read some more of NYT online, water*

02:01 P.M.–02:30 P.M.: *proofed ads—sent changes to ad dept., bathroom*

02:31 P.M.–03:00 P.M.: *called Jane about design project*

03:01 P.M.–03:30 P.M.: *spoke to Andre about budget, went to get coffee*

03:31 P.M.–04:00 P.M.: *called Jane back, left message w/new figure*

04:01 P.M.–04:30 P.M.: *interviewed candidate for Assistant position*

04:31 P.M.–05:00 P.M.: *talked to Andre about candidate—terrible!!!*

05:01 P.M.–05:30 P.M.: *read through resumes received from Monster*

05:31 P.M.–06:00 P.M.: *returned personal e-mails*

06:01 P.M.–06:30 P.M.: *haircut*

06:31 P.M.–07:00 P.M.: *haircut*

07:01 P.M.–07:30 P.M.: *met Liz for dinner*

07:31 P.M.–08:00 P.M.: *dinner*

08:01 P.M.–08:30 P.M.: *dinner*

08:31 P.M.–09:00 P.M.: *train home*

09:01 P.M.–09:30 P.M.: *home—looked through catalogs*

09:31 P.M.–10:00 P.M.: *checked baseball game*

10:01 P.M.–10:30 P.M.: *watched baseball game & talked to Mark*

10:31 P.M.–11:00 P.M.: *washed face, brushed teeth*

11:01 P.M.–11:30 P.M.: *read novel*

11:31 P.M.–12:00 A.M.: *sleep*

12:01 A.M.–12:30 A.M.: *sleep*

12:31 A.M.–01:00 A.M.: *sleep*

01:01 A.M.–01:30 A.M.: *sleep*

01:31 A.M.–02:00 A.M.: *sleep*

02:01 A.M.–02:30 A.M.: *sleep*

02:31 A.M.–03:00 A.M.: *sleep*

03:01 A.M.–03:30 A.M.: *sleep*

03:31 A.M.–04:00 A.M.: *sleep*

04:01 A.M.–04:30 A.M.: *sleep*

04:31 A.M.–05:00 A.M.: *sleep*

05:01 A.M.–05:30 A.M.: *sleep*

05:31 A.M.–06:00 A.M.: *sleep*

ACTIVITY LOG EVALUATION WORKSHEET

Once you've completed seven Activity Log Worksheets in a row (one for each day), evaluate them carefully to determine exactly how you're spending your time. Calculate how much time you spend each week doing various important, critical, and time-wasting activities. The following examples of work and personal activities should help you get started in figuring out exactly how much time you spend doing various things each week.

WORK RELATED ACTIVITIES

Commuting To/From Work

_____ Hours Per Day x _____ Days Per Week=Total Hours Spent:_____

Reading Mail/E-mail

_____ Hours Per Day x _____ Days Per Week=Total Hours Spent:_____

Talking on the Phone

_____ Hours Per Day x _____ Days Per Week=Total Hours Spent:_____

Sitting in Meetings

_____ Hours Per Day x _____ Days Per Week=Total Hours Spent:_____

Performing Important Work-Related Tasks

_____ Hours Per Day x _____ Days Per Week=Total Hours Spent:_____

Performing Unimportant Work-Related Tasks

_____ Hours Per Day x _____ Days Per Week=Total Hours Spent:_____

Dealing with Unexpected Interruptions

_____ Hours Per Day x _____ Days Per Week=Total Hours Spent:_____

Dealing with Unexpected Emergencies

_____ Hours Per Day x _____ Days Per Week=Total Hours Spent:_____

Doing Paperwork/Completing Reports

_____ Hours Per Day x _____ Days Per Week=Total Hours Spent:_____

Time Spent Working Specifically Toward Work-Related Goals

_____ Hours Per Day x _____ Days Per Week=Total Hours Spent:_____

Other Task:_____

_____ Hours Per Day x _____ Days Per Week=Total Hours Spent:_____

Other Task:_____

_____ Hours Per Day x _____ Days Per Week=Total Hours Spent:_____

Other Task:_____

_____ Hours Per Day x _____ Days Per Week=Total Hours Spent:_____

Other Task:_____

_____ Hours Per Day x _____ Days Per Week=Total Hours Spent:_____

Other Task:_____

_____ Hours Per Day x _____ Days Per Week=Total Hours Spent:_____

PERSONAL ACTIVITIES

Cooking/Eating

_____ Hours Per Day x _____ Days Per Week=Total Hours Spent:_____

Sleeping

_____ Hours Per Day x _____ Days Per Week=Total Hours Spent:_____

Personal Grooming

_____ Hours Per Day x _____ Days Per Week=Total Hours Spent:_____

Cleaning/Laundry

_____ Hours Per Day x _____ Days Per Week=Total Hours Spent:_____

Driving

_____ Hours Per Day x _____ Days Per Week=Total Hours Spent:_____

Spending Quality Alone Time

_____ Hours Per Day x _____ Days Per Week=Total Hours Spent:_____

Spending Quality Time with Loved Ones

_____ Hours Per Day x _____ Days Per Week=Total Hours Spent:_____

Reading (Books, magazines, newspapers, etc.)

_____ Hours Per Day x _____ Days Per Week=Total Hours Spent:_____

Watching TV

_____ Hours Per Day x _____ Days Per Week=Total Hours Spent:_____

Paying Bills/Doing Paperwork

_____ Hours Per Day x _____ Days Per Week=Total Hours Spent:_____

Running Errands

_____ Hours Per Day x _____ Days Per Week=Total Hours Spent:_____

Participating in a Hobby (for pleasure)

_____ Hours Per Day x _____ Days Per Week=Total Hours Spent:_____

Time Spent Pursuing Personal Goals

_____ Hours Per Day x _____ Days Per Week=Total Hours Spent:_____

Other Activity

_____ Hours Per Day x _____ Days Per Week=Total Hours Spent:_____

Other Activity

_____ Hours Per Day x _____ Days Per Week=Total Hours Spent:_____

Other Activity

_____ Hours Per Day x _____ Days Per Week=Total Hours Spent:_____

Other Activity

_____ Hours Per Day x _____ Days Per Week=Total Hours Spent:_____

Other Activity

_____ Hours Per Day x _____ Days Per Week=Total Hours Spent:_____

....

....

Are you involved in organizations, associations, clubs, or other activities that are not contributing to your career advancement and that don't provide an adequate social or recreational outlet? If so, seriously consider dropping these activities in order to give yourself more time to focus on what's important.

....

Next, study your surroundings both at work and at home. At work, for example, how could furniture and office equipment be reorganized or moved around to create a better and more productive work environment? Are the items and papers you use constantly conveniently located at or near your desk, or do you spend a lot of time looking for papers, items, or information you need? Are the phone numbers of the people you call regularly readily accessible? Is the lighting and temperature in your office conducive to helping you be productive and concentrate?

Based on the activity log you create and the evaluation of your workspace, what needs to be changed? How could you modify your work habits and how you spend your time to make yourself more productive and less stressed?

Using the method of prioritizing activities described in the last chapter, take each item or task you spend time doing and categorize it using the A, B, C, 1, 2, 3 system. Also, by preplanning your activities, you'll be able to better deal with unexpected situations as they arise, because contingency plans will already be in place. This will help eliminate stress and boost your productivity.

....

As you allocate time to accomplish various tasks, don't forget to factor in time to deal with interruptions and unexpected emergencies. Make sure you never totally book up your day. If something suddenly arises that requires your attention, you should have unscheduled time already factored into your schedule to deal with it, without causing you to fall too far behind on your other responsibilities or work.

....

After you've discovered exactly how you spend your time, you need to adopt some type of time management tool to help you better plan your day and stay focused. The last section of this chapter describes various traditional (paper-based), electronic, and online time management tools currently available to you. Choose one that best fits your personal and professional habits.

Time Saving and Organizational Tips

The general strategies for maximizing your time include:

- Evaluating how you use your time
- Focusing your time on priorities and important tasks

- Planning how your time will be utilized
- Figuring out how to use your existing time more effectively
- Eliminating time wasters
- Avoiding distractions
- Improving your basic skill set so you can more easily accomplish work related tasks faster and more accurately
- Determining how much your time is worth and maximizing your "costs"

Maintain a sense of flexibility. Unexpected events and issues will arise often. Be prepared to deal with these issues and have contingency plans already in place. Between 30 and 40% of your time should not be pre-scheduled, however, so that you'll be able to deal with unexpected interruptions, emergencies, and other issues that arise throughout your day.

The following are some basic tips for helping you become better organized and adopt improved time management techniques into your daily work routine:

- As you begin to utilize the time management tool you choose to adopt, set aside a predefined amount of time (15 minutes should be adequate) at the same time each day to plan out your day. The best time to do this is first thing in the morning, when you get to work or during your commute to work (if you take a train or carpool, for example).
- Once you adopt your time management tool, use it in every aspect of your life and keep all your plans (personal and professional) in one place. Keeping a separate schedule for your personal and professional life can get confusing and could result in accidentally double booking your time.
- Part of your daily schedule should include a "To-Do" list of the day's major activities and objectives. This could include important calls you need to make, letters you need to write, errands you need to complete, and work or personal related tasks that need to get accomplished that day. Once the basic "To-Do" list is written, take a few moments to prioritize each

item on the list, again using the A, B, C, 1, 2, 3 method. You'll want to focus your peak time (the time of the day when you're the most alert and productive) to completing the top (most important) three to five items on your list.

- As soon as you determine what the most important activities of the day are, add them to your schedule and allocate the necessary time in your day to accomplish them. Also, allocate non-prime hours of your workday to accomplish paperwork and other less critical tasks. Schedule time to do these activities and deal with them only during that allocated time.

- Most organizational experts agree that when dealing with paperwork, you should never handle the same piece of paper twice. When you receive a memo, report, or other document and handle it for the first time, don't just file it away for later review. Do what needs to be done and get rid of the paper. Don't allow it to clutter your office or workspace. Maintain "In" and "Out" boxes to handle documents as you deal with them. Make sure you do something with every piece of paper that crosses your desk. Don't just place it back on a pile or move it from one pile to another.

- Learn to determine what papers are important and which can be filed away or discarded.

- Develop a productive way of promptly handling routine requests so that they don't take up too much of your time.

- Utilize some form of contact management software or PDA to keep an updated database of personal and business contacts. You should never need to waste time looking for someone's name, address, or phone number, or have to sort through hundreds or thousands of business cards to find whomever you're looking for. Once a contact is placed in your contact database or PDA, file their business card away, or discard it. (Make sure, however, you back up your contact database regularly.)

- Create a traditional or electronic filing system that allows you to quickly and easily find the information you're looking for.

You should never have to waste valuable time tracking down a file or looking for documents that have been misplaced.

- Learn how to delegate responsibilities and tasks that can help you free up your time and reduce work for which your particular skills, experience, and knowledge aren't required. For example, subordinates can be assigned to gather facts; prepare rough drafts of letters and reports; make photo-copies or handle printing and collating; sort through mail (or e-mail); screen incoming calls and voice mail messages; handle data entry; run errands; and handle tasks that are not part of your core competency.

- Some coworkers or superiors may become delegation happy. In other words, these people will attempt to delegate all their responsibilities to others to reduce or eliminate their own workload. It's in your best interest to learn how to say "no" when it's appropriate, so that you have ample time to focus on your own responsibilities. There will be times when it's in your best interest to take on additional responsibilities, but before doing this, make sure you have the time available.

When delegating a task, make sure you assign the right person to the job. Focus on obtaining the desired results, but don't necessarily dictate how something should get done (providing the desired result will ultimately be achieved). Trust the person you assign to do a task to handle it without you having to look over his or her shoulder. Provide a deadline and seek out periodic updates or progress reports as necessary. Be sure to provide feedback and praise often.

- Meetings can often become a major time waster at work. If you're in a position to do so, you can save substantial time by better organizing your meetings in advance. Determine what items need to be covered, for example, and then spell out (in writing) what you expect from the meeting's participants. Have a desired goal or outcome for the meeting and establish a way of measuring the results. To insure that peo-ple come to the meeting and are prepared, distribute a print-ed agenda with the purpose of the meeting clearly stated. Also, set a start and finish time for the meeting, and spell out what information or preparation for which each attendee is responsible.

- Once you determine how much your time is worth, focus on using that time to your utmost advantage. For example, if you bill out your time to clients at $50.00 per hour, don't waste your time making photocopies when you can pay someone only $10 per hour, for example, to do these tasks.

- Know the difference between urgent tasks that have short-term consequences and important tasks that you determine will have long-term implications that will also help you to reach your goals. This will help you properly categorize your "To-Do" list so that your focus is on achieving what's truly important as well as time sensitive.

JUGGLING YOUR PERSONAL AND PROFESSIONAL LIFE

No matter what you do for a living, one of the biggest challenges people face, especially in today's fast-paced world, is that they can't properly juggle their personal and professional lives. As a result, one's personal life (for example, spending quality time with loved ones) often gets forfeited in favor of professional obligations and responsibilities.

Based on your personal situation and what your various obliga-tions are, you may be willing to sacrifice some or all of your person-al life in favor of moving your career forward. If you're married and have children, however, it becomes much more important to prop-erly juggle your personal and professional life.

As you plan your schedule, be sure you allocate time to spend with your friends and family. You'll also want to set aside time for yourself. When you plan your personal and professional goals and begin scheduling your time, this is when you'll need to begin thinking about how to best manage all of your obligations. For each person, however, what percentage of time you spend pursuing personal versus professional interests will vary. Once again, as you actually experience your day-to-day living, be flexible. Issues will arise at work that require your attention, just as social plans will come up in which you'll want to participate.

To better live a stress-free life that makes you truly happy, you'll need to develop a system for properly juggling your personal and professional life. Ideally, you never should feel guilty focusing your attention on one area of your life, even when your attention should really be focused elsewhere.

MAXIMIZE YOUR DOWN TIME

Having down time during your day is the perfect opportunity to relax, take your mind off work-related issues, and regroup, even if it's only for a few minutes at a time. If you have downtime when commuting to and from work, however, you can take this opportunity to:

- Make phone calls (via cellular phone) when safe and respectful of others
- Review voice mail messages (via cellular phone)
- Hold teleconferences (via cellular phone) when safe and respectful of others
- Surf the Web (using a wireless modem and a laptop, or a wireless PDA, such as the Palm VII or Palm V with OmniSky service)
- Listen to books on tape (either educational or entertaining)
- Read the newspaper or magazines to keep up-to-date on current events
- Read trade journals to keep up on industry-oriented news
- Dictate memos and reports using a cassette recorder
- Do your schedule planning for the day

Obviously, what you're able to do when commuting will depend on whether you drive yourself to work, carpool, take the train, walk, bike ride, or use some other form of public transportation.

The cost of having and using a cellular telephone has dropped dramatically in recent years. Companies, like Sprint PCS (www.sprintpcs.com), offer flat-rate digital cellular service with no roaming or long distance charges. For example, with Sprint PCS, you could spend $200.00 per month and receive 2,000 minutes of cellular phone service. (Much less expensive plans are also available.) This offers you plenty of time to conduct business that would otherwise need to wait until you're at your desk.

Based on the value of your time and the amount of time you'll be able to save by making calls during your commute, for example, you'll most likely be able to easily justify the cost of a cellular phone if you regularly commute to and from work. Of course, you must exercise common sense and basic courtesy when using a cellular phone on your commute. Never allow your cell phone calls to annoy fellow commuters on public transport or to distract you as you drive.

While traveling in the car, the radio is a wonderful tool for listening to news and keeping track of current events and listening to music is an excellent way to help you relax and unwind. But, if your car is equipped with a cassette or CD player, you can also use your commuting time to learn new skills or enjoy listening to a best-selling novel that you don't otherwise have time to read.

Courses on how to improve your reading speed, improve your memory, learn a foreign language, maximize your time, become a better public speaker, or better manage your money are just some of the things that can be learned—at your own pace—by listening to audio-based programs.

"Using a learning cassette, the listener has the perfect tool to review each basic idea presented over and over until he or she sees it, understands it and assimilates it. No other learning method can be used as easily and regularly," said Arnold Carter, vice president of communications research for Nightingale-Conant (800-647-9198 or www.nightingale.com) one of the leading publishers of instructional and self-help audio programs.

Every month, Audio-Tech Business Book Summaries (800-776-1910 or www.audiotech.com) offers an audiocassette program that summarizes two business books in between 30 and 40 minutes each. The Audio-Tech Business Book Summaries service is offered on an annual subscription basis and is designed to help busy business executives stay up-to-date on the latest business trends and learn new skills that will help them stay competitive, no matter what type of business they're in.

If you're more interested in listening to an unabridged how-to or self-help book or a popular novel, Simon & Schuster Audio (www.simonsays.com/audio) offers an extensive catalog of audio books which are sold at bookstores.

"Some people listen to fiction in order to relax. Others prefer to be more productive with their time by listening to non-fiction in order to gain knowledge or learn new skills. One of the most common places people listen to audio books is in their car," said Seth Gershel, senior vice president and publisher for Simon & Schuster Audio. "Many people get so engrossed in audio books, they actually begin to wish their commute were longer."

Using a microcassette recorder while sitting in traffic, many people boost their overall productivity by dictating letters and memos, keeping track of ideas when they can't write them down, or to recite a daily to-do list on their way to work.

Nobody enjoys being stuck in traffic, especially after a long and hard day at work, but if you have to commute, it's important to find innovative ways to make the most out of your time in the car. To avoid getting into an accident, however, never attempt to read or write while driving, and use caution while using a cellular phone and driving. Some regions are legislating against using a cell phone while driving, so be aware of your area's laws on this matter. Eating in the car can also be a distraction, which could result in an auto accident if you're not careful.

TIME MANAGEMENT AND ORGANIZATIONAL TOOLS

Developing goals and planning your time should all be done in writing. If you're at all technologically savvy, tapping the power of a personal digital assistant (PDA), scheduling (or "personal information management") software on a computer, or an online-based scheduling application can be extremely beneficial, as you'll find out in this section.

If you're not interested in using technology to help you become a better organized person, there are many different types of traditional (printed) planners or calendars that can be extremely useful. Companies like Day-Timer, Inc., and Franklin Covey are dedicated to helping people take advantage of time management tools to get the most of their time.

The following are descriptions of just some of the many different types of scheduling and organizational tools available. Many of these tools are inexpensive and will pay for themselves many times over as you begin using any one of them to help you maximize your time.

Traditional Planners

A traditional (printed) planner is typically comprised of a binder containing various specially designed pages that will help you plan your time, manage "To-Do" lists, keep track of expenses, and plan your goals. Two of the best known companies that manufacture traditional planners in a wide range of styles and formats are Day-Timer, Inc., and Franklin Covey.

The planners developed by these two companies can be purchased from office supply superstores, online, or via mail order. Franklin Covey also has its own chain of retail stores located in malls throughout America.

Day-Timer, Inc.

(800-225-5005/www.daytimer.com)

Day-Timer, Inc., offers a wide range of paper-based time management and organizational tools and systems. In addition to computer software (described later), the company offers loose-leaf and wirebound planners in a multitude of sizes to accommodate an individual's needs.

In addition to offering different sized planners, the company also offers different page layouts, including the following formats:

Two-Pages-Per-Week
One-Page-Per-Day
Two-Pages-Per-Day

The Two-Pages-Per-Week format allows someone to scan their entire week. Each page offers areas for a "To-Do" list, appointments and diary. Weekday hours run from before 8:00 A.M. to 6:00 P.M.. The binder is designed to hold six months worth of pages at a time.

The One-Page-Per-Day format offers space on each page to plan out one entire day. The daily schedule area of the page runs from 8:00 A.M. to 9:00 P.M., plus there's room for a "To-Do" list and expenses.

For the maximum amount of planning space, the Two-Pages-Per-Day planner format allows anyone to keep detailed "To-Do" lists and plan their day between 8:00 A.M. and 6:00 P.M., with plenty of extra room for jotting down notes and other important information.

· ·

Before adopting a personal planner, be sure to examine the various page layouts available to you and choose the format that best meets your needs, based on your own schedule and work habits. You can easily see samples the various types of planners at any office supply superstore, or you can request that sample planner pages be sent to you directly from the various manufacturers. The websites for companies like Day-Timer, Inc., and Franklin Covey also display sample planner page layouts.

· ·

....

If you choose to use a traditional printed planner to handle your
scheduling needs, be sure you write either in pencil or very neatly
in pen, so that you can easily read your own writing and make
changes as needed throughout your day.

....

Franklin Covey
(800-819-1812 /www.franklincovey.com)

Time management and personal planning tools developed by
Franklin Covey are used by over 15 million people worldwide. In
addition, the company teaches its time management techniques to
over 750,000 individuals each year through training seminars held
throughout the country. There are also more than 130 Franklin
Covey retail stores nationwide that sell the company's products,
which are also available from office supply superstores, via mail
order or online from the company's website.

Like Day-Timer, Inc., Franklin Covey offers many different printed planners in different sizes. A wide range of binder styles and
page layouts are also available to help people develop the perfect
time management tool to meet their individual and professional
needs. The company also offers several high-tech time management
tools that take advantage of desktop computer, Internet, and/or
PDA technology.

Electronic Organizers (PDAs)

Palm PDAs
(www.palm.com)

Palm Computing, Inc., is the manufacturer of the most popular
hand-held personal digital assistants in the worlds. The Palm OS
(operating system) dominates almost 80% of the PDA market.

In addition to having a powerful built-in scheduling program built into every Palm PDA, these units also contain a built-in contact management program, calculator, memo pad, expense calculator/tracker, clock, and the ability to sync information with a desktop computer. There are also over 5,000 optional programs that can be added to the Palm PDA units, making them even more powerful and versatile.

At the time this book was written, the Palm product line consisted of models ranging in price from $149.00 (the Palm M100) to $399 (Palm Vx and Palm VII). While all the Palm units have the same basic build-in applications, the more expensive units offer a smaller size, more internal memory, wireless communication capabilities, and/or better quality screens.

All of these units are battery powered, can be used virtually anywhere. From a size standpoint, they easily fit into the palm of your hand, within a shirt or jacket pocket, or within a purse or briefcase. At the touch of a button, not only will you have access to your complete schedule, you can also look up names, addresses, and phone numbers; write notes to yourself; send/receive e-mail; or surf the Web (wirelessly or using a traditional modem, depending on the Palm model).

One of the best features of these powerful hand-held units is that information between the Palm and any PC or Macintosh can be exchanged in seconds using one-button synchronization. Information can easily be transferred between popular time management and contact management programs, such as Act! 2000, Outlook 2000, Lotus Organizer, SideKick, and other programs. Text documents, spreadsheet data, database entries, and e-mail messages can also be transferred quickly, so a vast amount of information can be carried with you anytime, anywhere.

In addition to thousands of add-on programs that allow people to customize their Palm to handle a wide range of tasks, a selection of optional accessories are also available. Wireless modems, traditional modems, GPS (global positioning system) receivers, portable digital cameras, MP3 players, full-size keyboards, and travel cases are available to enhance the power and capabilities of these PDA units.

The Palm OS operating system has also been licensed by other

PDA manufacturers, including HandSpring, which offers its own line of Visor PDAs (www.handspring.com).

Whether you use a Palm alone, or in conjunction with a desktop computer, software applications (such as Act! 2000, Franklin Planning Software, or Day-Timer 2000 software), the Palm PDAs offer the power of a computer and the availability of a vast amount of information in the palm of your hand. The units are also relatively easy to use, especially if you already have basic computer knowledge.

Franklin Covey's *What Matters Most* time management program has been adapted into a software package designed specifically for the Palm PDAs. This program is designed to teach people how to become more organized, set goals and priorities, reduce stress in their lives, gain more confidence, and better organize critical information. For more information, call 800-236-5285 or visit the company's website at www.franklincovey.com. Special workshops that teach *What Matters Most* are offered nationwide.

Windows CE Palmtops (PDAs)

PalmPilots and other PDAs that use the Palm OS operating system may be among the most popular in the world, but a handful of companies, including Hewlett-Packard, Casio, and Compaq offer PDAs that use the Windows CE operating system. These units tend to be priced between $299.00 and $699.00, but have full-color LCD screens and operate using an interface that's very similar to Windows 98 (used on many desktop computers). These PDAs also offer built in scheduling/time management applications, along with other programs designed to make the user more productive and organized.

Computer Software

These days, millions of people have access to desktop computers. Personal Information Managers (PIMs) are software packages designed to handle a wide range of time management and organizational functions. Many of these programs offer powerful scheduling, electronic filing, and contact management modules, plus integrate email, fax technology, and the ability to link documents, created in programs such as Microsoft Word or Excel. The following are some of the more popular PIMs available for personal (desktop) computers. These packages can be purchased wherever software is sold or online.

- Act! 2000, Interact Commerce Corporation, www.act.com— Available for PC, Macintosh, Palm OS, and the Internet. This is an incredibly powerful, versatile, and customizable time management, organizational, and contact management tool.
- Microsoft Outlook 2000, Microsoft Corporation, www.microsoft.com—Available for PC-based computers running Windows 95, 98, or 2000. A version of this program comes with Microsoft Office as well as with the Microsoft Explorer Internet browser.
- Day-Timer Organizer 2000, Day-Timer, Inc., www.daytimer.com—Available for PC. This software takes the extremely popular Day-Timer planners and offers a digital version, which includes powerful time management and contact management applications.
- Franklin Planner Software for Windows, Franklin Covey, www.franklincovey.com—This software utilizes the time management and organizational techniques used in the company's printed planners, but adds additional functionality and versatility. This software features a multimedia presentation called *Discovering What Matters Most*, which teaches some of the company's most useful time management techniques. Data entered into this software can be synchronized

easily with a Palm OS-compatible PDA. A free, 30-day trial version of the software can be downloaded from the company's website.

- On Target 2.3 Software, Franklin Covey, www.franklincovey .com—This is powerful, yet easy-to-use project planning software. It's designed to walk you through the entire project planning process, plus generate professional quality reports.

Online Time Management and Organizational Tools

If you don't want to use an off-the-shelf software package on your personal computer or a PDA, there are a growing number of Internet-based time management applications available. The benefit of using any of these applications is that your schedule and data can be accessed from any device that connects to the Internet, whether it's a computer, PDA, or another Internet-compatible device. The majority of these online applications cost nothing to use, yet are extremely powerful planning tools.

- Franklin Planner Online (www.franklinplanner.com)—Track personal and group schedules; store all of your personal and business contact information; view daily, weekly and monthly calendars; use the Event Directory to track sports schedules, holidays, movie releases, and more; follow your financial portfolios; receive reminder and event notifications; receive weather forecasts and inspiring quotes for the day; and set up your own private discussion boards for your family, organization, or club(s). These are just some of the online applications available from this free service. Your customizable home page, when you use this service, displays your scheduled events, weather forecast for your location, your daily horoscope, and other personalized information. The information you add to the scheduling portion of this online application can be synchronized with a software package, such as Microsoft Outlook or Act! 2000, or with a personal digital assistant.

- Interact.com (www.interact.com)—The power of ACT! 2000 has been added to this online-based application, which can be accessed by any computer, PDA, or cellular phone that can access the Web. This is a powerful scheduling and contact management tool that can be used alone or in conjunction with Act! 2000 or Microsoft Outlook 2000. This application integrates scheduling, contact management, "To-Do" list management, file management, and e-mail.

- Day-Timer Digital (http://digital.daytimer.com)—Manage your schedule, address book, "To-Do" lists, and other information online using techniques and on-screen information gathering forms created based on Day-Timer's proven time management and organizational tools. View scheduling information in several different daily, weekly, and monthly formats. Data can be printed or transferred to any one of several popular PC-based software packages or to a PDA.

- Yahoo! Calendar (http://calendar.yahoo.com)—This is a simple (and free) scheduling application that is part of the Yahoo! Internet search engine. You can enter, view, and store appointments and scheduling information in a variety of daily, weekly, monthly, or yearly formats.

With proper planning, there is time in the day for you to excel in your professional life, but also to spend quality time with loved ones and/or have quality alone time. There's also time for you to pursue your various personal and professional goals, while at the same time, fulfilling your various other obligations.

By applying time management and organization skills to everything you do, you'll find your life will become less stressful, while you become more productive. Taking advantage of the time management and organization tools available to you will also help you better achieve your goals.

Now that you have established your personal, professional, and financial goals, and have a general idea on how to plan your time to make these goals a reality, you can begin focusing on your actual career path. The next chapter will help you to ensure the job(s) you accept in the future, will help you to fulfill your long-term professional goals, while at the same time, helping to insure you'll be happy on the job and don't wind up in a dead-end job that's frustrating.

SUCCESS STORY:
Helen Organizes Her Time

HELEN HAD RECENTLY been promoted to a management position in the Voting Rights Division of the Justice Department. She had worked for the department for about three years, getting steady raises and increasing responsibility. As a manager she would be involved in planning for and implementing the redistricting that will result from the data collected in 2000 census.

Helen was delighted with her promotion. She was eager to have more input in running the department, especially at this crucial time. However, when she started in her new position she found that she was really struggling with her new responsibilities. She found the time she spent in meetings, interviewing prospective job candidates, and running the intern program left her with little of her work day left to attend to the day-to-day responsibilities of her new position.

Helen wasn't able to stay late because she was also attending law school at night, and needed to complete her work within the confines of her eight-hour day. Helen knew this was possible because the other managers didn't stay late and seemed to manage their workload. Helen analyzed her time. She realized that she was spending quite a bit of time preparing for meetings because she was new to the management team. She realized this would change as she became more comfortable in the position. She also realized that she was spending at least an hour interviewing each candidate, even when the candidates weren't especially strong. Helen decided to keep her interviews to half an hour. She also decided to spend less time mentoring the interns. At this point in her career, she realized that she needed to focus on getting her work done and still leave herself enough energy to concentrate on her law studies.

Helen's time was very limited, but her inclination as a person was to give other people as much of her time as they needed. As a manager, Helen was responsible for more people and she realized that she could not give each person who crossed her path unlimited amounts of her time. Helen learned to be more selective and limited with her time so that she could meet her own goals of succeeding in her new position while staying on track with her law school program.

CHAPTER 7

finding the job that's best suited for you

IT'S A FACT—those who tend to be extremely successful from a professional standpoint have developed a true passion for whatever it is they do. Because these people enjoy their work and continue to be challenged by it, they're eagerly willing to put their effort into every task they set out to accomplish.

What most successful people have done is find a way to focus on what they truly enjoy, plus determine what they're good at (what their strengths are), then leverage these talents into a career that allows them to earn a fruitful living. Because these people are doing work they enjoy, tapping their natural abilities and proficiencies, and thrive on the ongoing challenges they face each day, they don't become bored with the day-to-day work related activities with which they're involved. As a result, they're highly motivated, success oriented, and, most importantly, they're happy with their professional life. These people are truly passionate! Are you?

Unfortunately, few people can actually boast that they're truly happy about all aspects of their professional life. Being forced to work each day for the sole purpose of earning a paycheck is not the proper motivation for long-term success. People who know that their job responsibilities today will be the same tomorrow, next week, next month, and for as long as they hold their current job, tend to become bored, frustrated, and depressed. They also tend to lose whatever motivation they once had to achieve their goals, and wind up working hard, but achieving no long-term career-related rewards.

If you're stuck in a dead-end job right now or you're looking to change jobs (in hopes of moving your career forward), this chapter will help you find a job that makes the most of your abilities, engages your creativity, and rewards you on many levels

DEFINING YOUR LONG-TERM CAREER PATH

Earlier in this book, you answered a lot of questions about what type of work you're good at, what you enjoy, and what type of work you'd ultimately enjoy doing. You were also asked about what type of work environment in which you'd prefer to be, what type of people you'd like your coworkers to be, and what type of work schedule enhances your productivity.

You were also asked to write a detailed job description of your dream job. Now, as you begin to create a career path for yourself, the answers you developed earlier should be taken into consideration. You may want to revisit your responses and make sure you were perfectly honest in your responses. There is no "right" dream job, only the type of job that would be perfect for you.

Developing a career path for yourself can be done anytime—while you're still in school, just after you graduate, or after you've gained years worth of professional experience. The purpose of defining a career path is to help you determine, in an organized and well-thought-out manner, where you are today from a professional standpoint, and where you ultimately want to be just before you retire.

Where you are right now professionally is the starting point in your career path. Determine exactly what your qualifications are, where your interests lie, what experience you have, what specific skills you already possess, and what types of positions you could fill today based upon your qualifications. You'll want to figure out exactly what you can offer to a potential employer and what your true earning potential is right now.

Your earning potential is based on a wide range of criteria, including your experience, skills, education, geographic area, the licenses or degrees you possess, and who your employer is.

As you define what your overall qualifications are and determine what types of jobs you could fill, you also want to consider what types of jobs you'd enjoy doing and consider what aspects of the job are most likely to hold your interest and keep you motivated over time.

Once you know what type of job you're capable of landing right now, you also want to develop long-term career-related goals in order to determine where you want your career to lead in the future—5, 10, 15, and 20 years down the road.

By the time you retire, where you do want your career path to have taken you? What is your ultimate professional goal or aspiration? With the starting point being right now and the ending point in your career being where you want to be at your retirement, you'll then want to create a timeline that fills in the blanks between the starting and ending points of your career path.

What will it take for you to reach your ultimate career goals, based on where you are right now? What types of promotions will you need to earn over time? What new skills will you need to acquire or develop? What new job titles will you have to earn? For which employers will you most likely need to work?

Unless you're working for your family business or starting your own company, chances are you'll have to work your way up to positions of greater responsibility. You'll need to constantly take on new responsibilities, earn promotions, and prove yourself to your current employer, or new employers, in order to keep your career path moving forward. This is what's necessary to eventually achieve your career goals. Doing this properly will take hard work and proper planning. It will also require you to always be on the lookout for new opportunities, and when you stumble upon an opportunity, to take full advantage of it.

By devising a long-term career path, you'll always have a new job title or promotion to be working toward, because you'll have a defined direction in which you want your career to lead. Knowing where you want to go and understanding what it will take to get there will help you stay motivated and ultimately achieve your objectives. This is what following a career path is all about.

In some large corporations, your career path will be more or less defined for you. In order to reach a certain level within the corporate hierarchy, you'll need to first meet the qualifications and hold specific positions. In these situations, simply putting in the time and hard work (and demonstrating dedication to the employer) will probably allow you to keep your career path moving forward.

There are many situations, however, when in order to achieve a career objective that you define for yourself, there will be no career path laid out for you. This will require you to develop your own career path based on what you believe you need to accomplish in order to achieve your ultimate goals.

When your career path needs to be self-charted, which is increasingly the norm, it's important to develop a thorough understanding of what you're ultimately trying to achieve and then define the specific steps you'll need to take in order to reach your destination. Each new responsibility you take on, each promotion you earn, and each new job you accept, you should be taking a clearly defined step forward—toward your ultimate career objective. Taking lateral career steps can be beneficial at times because these jobs will often help you to expand your skill set, even though your compensation or job title may remain constant. As you evaluate each career-related decision you make, ideally it should clearly demonstrate a forward moving career path or somehow benefit your career overall.

CAN YOUR CURRENT JOB LEAD YOU WHERE YOU WANT TO GO?

Once you determine where you are right now (today) in terms of your career path, the next step is to evaluate your current job to determine if it's a stepping stone leading to future success or if it's a dead-end employment situation.

If you believe career advancement is possible with your current employer, ask yourself questions like:

- Does your employer offer on-the-job training that would qualify you for more advanced or higher-level positions?
- Is it possible for you to be promoted (and earn a pay increase) within your company?
- If a promotion (and raise) is possible, what would it take to obtain it?
- In what timeframe would you qualify for a raise or promotion?
- What steps need to be taken, starting now, for you to obtain a raise and/or promotion?
- Will the promotion lead you a step closer to achieving your long-term career objective? If so, how?

There are a handful of ways to quickly determine if you're currently stuck in a dead-end job. If you've been in the same job with the same employer for at least six months, and some or all of the following situations apply, chances are you're in a position with little or no career advancement potential:

- You have been offered no additional job responsibilities.
- You have been offered no on-the-job training.
- No discussion of career advancement has happened pursuant to an employee evaluation.
- Every day is basically the same in terms of your daily responsibilities.

If you believe you're in a dead-end job, you have several choices. You can stay where you are knowing there is no chance for advancement, promotions, or raises. In this situation, you may, however, have job security and a steady paycheck, which should allow you to meet all of your financial obligations. Chances are, you have already mastered all the skills needed to meet your job's responsibilities, so the stress levels associated with doing your job are minimal. The drawback to this scenario is that everyday you're on the job, your responsibilities and how you spend your time, are basically the same. You'll face few or no work-related challenges, and there is no chance of earning a raise or promotion. What your employer's expectations are today will be exactly what is expected of you one year from now, for example.

Assuming that being in a stagnant job isn't too attractive to you and there are future career-related goals you hope to achieve, being in a dead-end job now may be a roadblock, but it's not necessarily a permanent barrier holding you back.

Once you identify the limited potential of your job, you can make a conscious effort to change the situation. One thing you can do immediately is to meet with your employer and express a sincere interest in career advancement opportunities within the company for which you currently work. Determine what opportunities, if any, exist. If no opportunities exist, even once additional education or training is obtained, you'll need to begin a job search for other opportunities offering career advancement in the future and a possibly higher paycheck right now.

As your new job search begins, one of the biggest mistakes you can make is accepting another dead-end job, especially once you have long-term career goals in place. The easiest way to ensure you won't wind up in an employment situation that isn't beneficial to your career, take the following precautions:

- Do research. Learn as much as you can about a potential employer before participating in a job interview. Make sure the company with the job opening is one that you'd be interested in working for and that the work environment is suitable for you.
- Based on your company research, ask plenty of questions during the job interview(s).
- Ask for a detailed job description for the position for which you're applying. Determine exactly what the employer is looking for, what their expectations are, and what it will take for you to succeed in the position.
- Whenever possible, speak directly with other employees at the company (your potential coworkers). Are these people with whom you'd enjoy working?
- In the process of doing research and participating in job interviews, ask questions about work hours, job responsibilities, what a typical work day would be like, whom you'd be expected to answer to, and gather other pertinent information.
- As you learn about the position that's available, ask how you (as an employee) will be evaluated. Also, determine what type of on-the-job training will be offered, what it will eventually take to earn a promotion and/or pay raise, and what type of career advancement opportunities are available with the company. If you'll need additional training or education in order to become qualified for a higher-level job down the road, will it be provided and/or paid for by the employer?
- On a day-to-day basis, will the job you're applying for keep you interested and challenged? Will the position allow you to fully utilize your skills?

During the job interview process, it's best to hold off discussions about compensation, benefits, and perks until after the potential employer has expressed a strong interest in hiring you.

YOUR NEXT CAREER STEP

After evaluating your current employment situation, you may determine it's time to leave your current job in order to pursue another position. If this is the case, the first step is to begin updating your resume and evaluate your responses to the questions posed earlier in this book. Determine specifically what types of positions you're currently qualified to fill and what type of job you believe you'd prosper and in which you'd be happy. You also need to evaluate your own personal skill set, experience, and education, then determine what sets you apart from other job seekers. Take some time to answer these questions in as much detail as you can. While you've already answered questions similar to these earlier in the book, you may find that you've gained some new insight. You'll need to provide quantitative and qualitative answers to these questions, and at the same time, provide proof you posses the specific skills, education and work experience for which the potential employers are looking.

What specific skills make you marketable? _____

_____

_____

_____

What will employers most like about you?   _____

_____

_____

_____

What value can you offer to a potential employer? _____

_____

_____

_____

Before you actually begin searching for a new job, you'll need to know exactly what type of job you're actually looking for and determine for what you're qualified. If you begin applying for jobs you're not qualified to fill, your efforts will be futile.

Once you know what type of job you're qualified to fill and what type of job you'd like to land, the next step is to begin looking for the best possible opportunities—hopefully job opportunities that offer future career advancement opportunities that will ultimately lead you toward your goals.

FINDING THE BEST JOB OPPORTUNITIES

Your dream job is out there. What you'll find, however, is that upwards of 70 to 80% of all job openings are never advertised. To actually find the best opportunities, you'll need to do a lot more than blindly send out your resumes to potential employers and respond to "help wanted" ads. (Blindly sending out your resume refers to sending your resume to an employer whom you've never met and who hasn't specifically requested it.)

Finding the best job is a time consuming process. The more time you invest, however, the more exciting opportunities you'll find and the greater number of choices you'll have when it comes to actually choosing which opportunities to apply for and later accept.

Your job search efforts should involve taking a multifaceted approach. Instead of just relying on "help wanted" ads from your local newspaper, you'll also want to tap the power of the Internet, network, contact employment agencies (headhunters), and take advantage of every other resource you have available.

The best time to look for (and apply for) a new job is when you're still employed. This gives you plenty of time to make educated career decisions and not have to worry about from where your next paycheck will come. If you become desperate (because you're unemployed and have no money coming in), you'll feel pressure to accept the first job offer that comes along. This may not be the best possible opportunity to pursue, however.

If you're unemployed and desperate for cash to meet your financial obligations, to give yourself more time to find the best full-time career opportunities, seriously consider taking advantage of part-time employment opportunities available from temporary employment agencies. You will be able to earn a paycheck, yet maintain a flexible schedule, and have time to interview for full-time positions. You'll also have the opportunity to get your foot in the door and prove yourself to potential employers by working as a temp. It's a very common trend for companies to offer temporary employees, hired through an agency, a full-time job if the person proves to be competent, hard working, and qualified. One common misconception is that temp work typically involves low level clerical or data entry work, for example. In reality, companies hire temp workers to fill a wide range of positions for days, weeks, or sometimes months at a time.

Taking advantage of temporary employment opportunities to bring in an income during the job search process and also to get your foot in the door with an employer you'd potentially like to work for full-time is something many job seekers overlook.

The very best way to find the ideal job opportunity for you is through word-of-mouth via networking. This means that you speak with people you know, who work in your profession or industry (or who know people who do), and seek out personal recommendations and introductions to potential employers.

If someone you know works for a company you too would like to work for, having that personal acquaintance make an introduction on your behalf can be extremely useful, especially if the person making the introduction is considered to be a valuable and respected employee. Employers tend to trust their valued employees and take recommendations and applicant referrals from these people seriously.

TRADITIONAL JOB SEARCH METHODS

For most people, the job search process is something that's endured only a handful of times during one's professional life. This process cannot only be time consuming, it can also be stressful. The most obvious (and one of the easiest) method of finding job opportunities to apply for is to simply pick up a copy of your local newspaper and respond to a handful of "help wanted" ads.

While this method of finding jobs should not be overlooked, other traditional job search methods include:

- Contacting headhunters
- Attending job fairs
- Seeking the assistance of employment agencies
- Visiting the job placement office at your high school, college, or university
- Cold calling and then sending out your resume to the human resources department of companies you'd like to work for, even if those companies aren't advertising job openings.

USING THE INTERNET AS A POWERFUL JOB SEARCH TOOL

In addition to using the methods listed in the previous section to find the best possible job opportunities, if you have access to the Internet, you have at your disposal an incredibly powerful job search tool. Using the Internet you can:

- Visit career-related websites to access thousands of job listings
- Research companies (potential employers)
- E-mail potential employers your resume/cover letter
- Visit the websites operated by companies for which you'd like to work

- Create and update a traditional printed resume and/or an electronic resume

The following are just a few of the online career-related websites that will help you create and/or enhance your resume, find job opportunities, and obtain additional career-related advice. In addition to the websites listed below, you can also use any Internet search engine (such as Yahoo!, Google, Excite, MSN.com, AOL.com, or AltaVista) to find additional career-related websites and online resources available to job seekers. Use search words or phrases like "Resume," "Resume Creation," "Career Advice," "Job Listings," or "Job Openings."

Also, be sure to visit websites that cater specifically to your occupation. The websites operated by professional organizations, industry associations, or industry trade journals can all be extremely useful resources. You'll also find that there are career-related websites that focus on very specific types of jobs, industries, or careers.

A few examples of the many Web pages dedicated to specific professions include: The Boston Bar Association (www.bostonbar.org), Professional Secretaries International Association (www.gvi.net/psi), and the National Association of Sales Professionals (www.nasp.com).

Some of the popular career-related websites that cater to a general audience of job seekers include:

- 1st Impressions Career Site—www.1st-imp.com
- 6-Figure Jobs—www.6figurejobs.com
- Advanced Career Systems—www.resumesystems.com/career/Default.htm
- America's Employers—www.americasemployers.com
- America's Job Bank—www.ajb.dni.us
- Best Jobs USA—www.bestjobsusa.com
- Career & Resume Management for the 21st Century—http://crm21.com
- Career Builder—www.careerbuilder.com

- Career Center—
  www.jobweb.org/catapult/guenov/res.html#explore
- Career Creations—www.careercreations.com
- Career Express—www.careerxpress.com
- Career Spectrum—www.careerspectrum.com/
  dir-resume.htm
- Career.com—www.career.com
- CareerMosaic—www.careermosaic.com
- CareerNet—www.careers.org
- CareerPath—www.careerpath.com
- CareerWeb—www.cweb.com
- College Central Network—http://employercentral.com
- Competitive Edge Career Service—
  www.acompetitiveedge.com
- Creative Professional Resumes—www.resumesbycpr.com
- First Job: The Website—www.firstjob.com
- First Resume Store International—www.resumestore.com
- Hot Jobs—www.hotjobs.com
- JobBank USA—www.jobbankusa.com
- JobLynx—www.joblynx.com
- JobSource—www.jobsource.com
- JobStar—jobsmart.org/tools/resume
- JobTrack—www.jobtrack.com
- Kaplan Online Career Center—www.kaplan.com
- Monster Board—www.monster.com
- National Business Employment Weekly Online—
  www.nbew.com
- Professional Association of Resume Writers—
  www.parw.com/homestart.html
- Proven Resumes—www.free-resume-tips.com
- Proven Resumes—www.provenresumes.com
- Quintessential Careers—
  www.quintcareers.com/resres.html
- Rebecca Smith's eResumes & Resources—
  www.eresumes.com
- Resumania—www.resumania.com

- Resume Broadcaster—www.resumebroadcaster.com
- Resume Magic—www.liglobal.com/b_c/career/res.shtml
- Resume Plus—www.resumepls.com
- Resume.com—www.resume.com
- Resumedotcom—www.resumedotcom.com
- Salary.com—www.salary.com
- Taos Careers—www.taos.com/resumetips.html
- The Boston Herald's Job Find—www.jobfind.com
- The Employment Guide's Career Web—
  www.cweb.com/jobs/resume.html
- The Wall Street Journal Careers—www.careers.wsj.com
- Vault.com—
  www.vaultreports.com/jobBoard/SearchJobs.cfm
- Yahoo Careers—careers.yahoo.com

If you want to research a specific job title or occupation, one of the best places to turn is the online edition of *The Occupational Outlook Handbook*, published by The Bureau of Labor Statistics (http://stats.bls.gov/ocohome.htm).

NETWORKING

Knowing that the majority of jobs aren't ever advertised, one of the very best ways to find opportunities is through networking. This means contacting people you know—personally or professionally—and asking about any job opportunities they know about and for which you might be qualified.

According to a survey conducted by Manchester, Inc. (www.manchesterUS.com), a career management and consulting firm, networking was the number one method through which executives found new jobs in 1999. The results of the survey stated, "Networking accounted for 56% of successful job searches, while executives search firms were successfully used by 18% of executives. This was followed by answering help wanted ads (14%), the Internet (5%), mailed inquiries (4%) and self-employment (3%)." For any level job search—even if you're looking for your first professional job—networking is a critical component of any job search.

Networking can take on many forms. While many consider it a skill, networking can be easily mastered, allowing virtually anyone with friends, family, (former) coworkers, and professional acquaintances to find the best job opportunities, simply by striking up conversations with people and asking for assistance and/or referrals.

Networking is one of the best ways to explore what many call the "hidden job market." As you begin your job search, contact people you know, starting with people currently working in the industry in which you hope to work.

From the people you network with, you can typically:

- Discover unadvertised job openings
- Get referrals for other people to speak with about possible job openings
- Get your foot in the door at a company by having someone make a personal introduction
- Learn about specific companies (potential employers)
- Meet others working in the industry that interests you
- Obtain a letter of recommendation
- Receive career advice and guidance

You can expand your circle of professional acquaintances by joining and becoming active in professional associations or by participating in Internet-based newsgroups and online-based mailing lists. Clients, customers, and other people you know from current or past jobs can also be incorporated into your networking circle and tapped when it comes to finding job opportunities.

If you're first starting to develop a network, some of the other people you should consider contacting include, in addition to friends, family, and professional contacts, can be found among:

- Accountants (with clients in a wide range of industries)
- Your high school or college alumni association
- Bankers
- Your local Chamber of Commerce
- Church friends/clergy
- College friends
- Past teachers/deans
- Commuting acquaintances
- Doormen/security guards at office buildings
- Employees of targeted company
- Exercise club acquaintances
- Lawyers

If you don't know anyone working in your particular industry, write down the names of between 10 and 25 friends, relatives, and acquaintances whom you could call, right now, in order to ask about job leads or assistance in finding a new job. Even if you call each person on your list and none of them is able to help you directly, you're virtually guaranteed that someone on your list will know someone else who can help you find and land the job for which you're looking. When you correspond with a network contact that isn't a close friend or relative, be sure to refresh that person's memory about how they know you and when and where you met.

If a friend tells you that one of their other friends can probably help you, make a point to first meet that person before asking for his or her assistance. Be sure to briefly explain to your network contact(s) exactly what type of job you're looking for, and provide them with a short summary of your most impressive work experience and/or skills. You want your contacts to know something about you, so they can speak highly of you to their superiors, coworkers, or people in their network of friends and associates.

Developing a network is an ongoing process. Even after landing a job, you'll find these people will prove beneficial throughout your career. When it comes to finding a new job, the people you know can be as important as your qualifications. Networking can be a powerful job search tool, and networking in cyberspace makes meeting new people with similar professional interests fast and easy.

In addition to contacting friends, relatives, former coworkers, past teachers or professors, previous bosses, clients, and business associates, you can use the Internet, and the major online services, as a networking tool. All the major online services, such as America Online, offer special interest groups and professional forums allowing people to communicate with each other by posting public and private messages about specific topics. Through these forums, you can meet new people with common interests, discuss issues, get questions answered, and possibly learn about job openings.

Live chat or conferencing areas, available through the major online services and the Internet, allow people to communicate in real-time by typing messages to each other. Within these virtual chat rooms, dozens of people can communicate about specific topics simultaneously. At any given time, literally hundreds of different chat sessions are taking place on the online services. Special events are also planned by forum leaders, which provide opportunities to participate in question-and-answer sessions with special guests, authors, and recognized experts in various fields and professions.

Job seekers should definitely not overlook networking opportunities in cyberspace. To get yourself online in order to access professional forums and participate in chat sessions, you'll need a computer that's equipped with a modem and specialized communications software. You'll also need to obtain membership to one of the major online services or access to the Internet via an Internet service provider (ISP). Membership fees for the various online services and access to the Internet range from free to $30.00 per month, usually for unlimited access. Some free ISPs include www.netzero.com and www.freeinternet.com, and more can be found by searching online using the criteria "free isp."

DON'T THINK IN TERMS OF TRADITIONAL
JOB DESCRIPTIONS

Everyone, including you, has his or her own skill set, educational background, and work experience that set them apart from others. As part of your job search related research, you'll want to evaluate your skill set and determine all the different job titles you're qualified to fill. Keep in mind, many jobs in various industries have the same qualifications, but the actual job titles used are different. This is particularly true when it comes to Internet-based jobs. For example, someone who works as a writer may also be fully qualified to fill a position as an online content developer or an online editor for a website.

More often than not, someone's job title doesn't begin to describe anything about the job itself. For example, the job title Manager doesn't explain what the person's responsibilities are, whom they manage, what they manage, what they have accomplished, what skills are required or anything else a potential employer might find useful. This is all information that a potential employer needs to know before they can make an educated decision about hiring you.

As you list your job titles on your resume, try to make them as descriptive as possible, so that someone who isn't necessarily familiar with your line of work will be able to determine what your strengths are as an applicant.

The *Occupational Outlook Handbook* (http://stats.bls.gov/oco-home.htm) is a nationally recognized source of career information, designed to provide valuable assistance to individuals making decisions about their future work lives. This is an excellent resource for understanding job titles and responsibilities, and determining how you can incorporate this information into your resume.

Once you know what a typical employer will be looking for, you can cater your resume directly to a company by incorporating keywords, industry buzzwords, and other lingo you know for which a potential employer is looking. Pay careful attention to the "Training, Other Qualifications and Advancement" section of *The Occupational Outlook Handbook*. Here you'll find a listing of specific skills, licenses, degrees, accreditations, etc., that are usually required to enter a given field. Ideally, your personal qualifications will match up nicely with what *The Occupational Outlook Handbook* lists as being required to land a job in the field in which you're interested.

Another way of gathering information to help you list appropriate job titles, skills, job-related responsibilities, etc., within your resume is to carefully read and evaluate the job description or "help wanted" ad provided by the potential employer for whom you'd like to work.

If the ad states the employer is looking for someone with three to five years experience working in a specific position, make sure your resume reflects this information. Likewise, if the ad states proficiency using Microsoft Office 2000, for example, as a job requirement, this too needs to be highlighted in your resume.

Make sure the job opening being advertised is specifically the one you position yourself to be qualified to fill. Specific job titles, educational backgrounds, skills, and so on, listed within your resume should all match up with what the employer is looking for. In many cases, this will require you to customize your resume so that it's targeted to a specific job offered by a specific employer.

If the "help wanted" ad or job description you're responding to doesn't contain enough detail, find five or ten other "help wanted" ads or job descriptions (from other employers), that are similar to the job for which you'd like to apply. Try to incorporate the buzzwords and pertinent information from those ads into your resume to ensure your resume markets you as a qualified candidate for the type of job you're hoping to fill.

. . . .

As you describe your past work experience within your resume, make sure the supporting information under each job title succinctly describes your responsibilities and accomplishments. Just listing an impressive job title won't capture the reader's attention, especially if the job title is generic. Manager, Secretary, Salesperson, and Analyst are all examples of generic job titles that

don't begin to convey to the reader what your responsibilities were, what skills were required, or what your accomplishments were when you held that specific job.

DEFINING YOUR CURRENT EARNING POTENTIAL AND VALUE

The greatest measure of success for any job search effort is whether or not you ultimately land a job based on the positions you apply for and the opportunities you pursue. To ensure the job you wind up accepting is financially rewarding, you'll want to determine exactly what you're worth in today's competitive job market.

Are you like many people, working too hard for too many hours per week, yet not getting paid what you believe you deserve? Since salaries and compensation packages are typically kept confidential within a company, it can be difficult to determine if you're getting paid what you truly deserve based on your experience, skills, education, and overall value to the company for which you work.

Whether you're looking for a new job, hoping to earn a raise, or you're convinced you're not getting paid what you're worth in your current job, there are things you can do to discover your own true earning potential.

Many things contribute to someone's salary and overall compensation package. Work experience, education, skills, the size of the company, the industry, the geographic location of the employer, demand, the number of hours you work, and your ability to negotiate the best possible salary and compensation package all help to determine what you get paid.

Once you know exactly what type of job you're looking to fill (or you currently fill), by doing some research you can determine what salary range someone holding a similar job title and responsibilities earns within your industry and/or geographic area. Using this information, you can then determine if you're currently earning less than what you're worth and take the necessary steps to either pursue a higher paying job or a raise.

No matter in what industry you work, it's possible to pinpoint average salaries paid by employers for specific jobs. One of the best resources for gathering current and accurate salary information is *The Occupational Outlook Handbook* (www.bls.gov/ocohome.htm) published by The Bureau of Labor Statistics.

The Occupational Outlook Handbook is available at most libraries, the career services office at most high schools, colleges and universities, as well as online. It can also be ordered for $49.00 by calling 202-512-1800. For each of the thousands of occupations covered, this directory describes the nature of the work, working conditions, employment opportunities, the job outlook (between 1998 and 2008), the earning potential or salary range, as well as information about related occupations.

On the Web, there are many research firms and other sources of salary information; however, when using these sources for research, it's important to determine where the information is derived from, whether or not it's current, and if the data applies to your industry, occupation and geographic area.

JobSmart (www.jobsmart.org/tools/salary/sal-prof.htm) is a free service that publishes profession-specific salary surveys online for over 60 professions, ranging from accounting to warehousing.

Salary Master is an independent company that represents Information Technology (IT) professionals during salary negotiations. The company's website (http://salarymaster.com) offers a collection of articles and information for people looking to determine what they're worth as an employee in the high-tech field.

If you're contemplating moving to another city, you can easily compare what you're earning in one city with what you could be making in another city doing the same type of work by visiting Yahoo!'s Salary Comparison website at http://verticals.yahoo.com/salary.

One of the very best online resources for determining your worth and what you should be earning is Salary.com (www.salary.com). This website offers the SalaryWizard, which, after you answer a few basic questions, will give you an accurate and timely salary range that someone with your qualifications in your geographic area should be earning. This is a free service that also offers detailed career-related advice on a wide range of compensation issues.

Through research, it's relatively easy to determine if you're getting paid less than you're worth in today's marketplace. Knowing exactly what you're worth will help you participate successfully in a salary negotiation with your current or future employer.

During the negotiation process, always let the employer make a first offer. Once an offer is made, never accept it on the spot. Tell the employer you need at least several hours or a full day to consider the offer. If you know an employer is doing well financially and is desperate to fill the position you're qualified to fill, you'll have the advantage in a salary negotiation.

Never use your personal financial situation as a reason for requesting more money. Comments like "I need more money to afford my mortgage, rent, or car payments," don't concern the employer. Instead, focus on the value you are offering to the company and be prepared to offer qualitative and quantitative information to back up your statements. By proving to an employer you're worth the salary you're seeking, your chances of receiving it increase dramatically.

If you've never participated in a salary negotiation, read a book on how to negotiate so you become familiar with various tactics employers use during the salary negotiation process. Never settle for earning less than what you know you deserve based on your research. Keep in mind, however, there's a big difference between earning what you're actually worth in today's marketplace and what you think you're worth.

DOCUMENTING YOUR SUCCESS

The job search process involves many steps, including finding job opportunities, doing research about specific employers, writing or updating your resume, applying for jobs (sending resumes to potential employers and completing job applications), participating in job interviews, participating in salary negotiations (once you're offered a job), and then actually accepting a job offer.

On your resume, in your cover letters, and when participating in job interviews, it's easy to make boastful comments to a potential employer about your past work experience, education, and skill set. But, what you tell an employer will have much greater impact if you're able to document your successes with written quantitative and qualitative proof. By documenting past successes and your value as an employee, a potential employer will be taking much less of a risk by hiring you if you can prove that once you're hired, you'll not only meet the job's responsibilities, but you'll be able to exceed expectations. Some examples might include letters of recommendation, samples of your writing, reports you've created, portfolios, sales figures, and so on.

Every piece of written documentation you provide to a potential employer, including your resume, cover letters, letters of recommendation, and other proof of your professional accomplishments should all help to position you as the best possible candidate for the position for which you're applying.

YOUR DREAM JOB IS OUT THERE

There are many job opportunities out there. By tapping your own creativity, doing extensive research, utilizing your networking skills, and taking full advantage of the resources available to you on the Internet, you should be able to find job opportunities that will be emotionally and financially rewarding. You should be able to find jobs that will allow you to meet your financial obligations, yet at the same time, meet the criteria you already determined are important.

Whatever you do, never accept any job opportunity unless you know exactly what you're getting into. Make sure the job really entails what the employer says it does, that it will fully utilize your skills, and that it can lead to the career advancement opportunities you have determined are important to you in order to achieve your long-term career goals.

Even if your job search efforts become stressful, time consuming and frustrating, it's critical that you make the commitment to yourself to put in whatever effort is necessary to find and land the job you know will ultimately make you happy. Taking short cuts in the job search process or simply accepting the first job offer you receive might ensure that you quickly become employed, but the job you accept might not be the one you're best suited for or that will allow you to reach your true earning potential.

Finding what you believe to be your dream job will become much easier once you set your long-term career-related goals and objectives.

SUCCESS STORY:
Nick Finds His Dream Job

NICK WANTED TO pursue a career as a magazine editor, a notoriously difficult career to break into. He had editorial experience from working for his college newspaper and his internship at a major magazine over the summer between
his junior and senior years. He spent the summer doing research for the editors.
He also got the chance to see first hand "a day in the life" of an editorial assistant, which consisted of a lot of administrative tasks and very little editorial work.

Nick was offered a job with the same major magazine when he graduated for
$35,000. At the same time he was offered a job at a start-up magazine as an
intern for $75 a week. Nick was faced with a tough decision.

Nick knew that his first priority was to get some real editorial experience. While
the pay was awful at the start-up, the job would allow him to work with, and learn
from, a very talented editor. At the major magazine, he would be handling the
administrative details of a busy editor's office and get very little mentoring. Nick's
financial goals were fairly modest. He just needed to find a way to live on his
salary.

When he considered his priorities, his decision became easier to make. He gave
up his studio and moved in with some friends who had a great deal on rent and
learned to live frugally. His job at the start-up magazine was a true learning experience and when the editor moved to another magazine, she brought Nick along.
Nick has worked his way up to becoming a top editor for a top magazine, and is
now, thankfully, making far more than $75 a week.

CHAPTER 8

developing your professional image and marketing yourself

WHO YOU ARE and how people perceive you is critical in the business world. Your appearance, attitude, reputation, on-the-job performance, and how you treat others all play a tremendous role in contributing to your overall image and ultimate success. Unfortunately, in today's business environment, rumors and people's perceptions of you (whether legitimate or not), also play a big role in how you're perceived.

There are basically two ways to get ahead in life. You can lie, cheat, and steal (and hopefully never get caught), or you can *always* act ethically, be honest and work hard for your success. Using the first approach, everything you obtain as a lying, thieving, backstabber can be instantly taken away when (not if) you're caught. If you work hard for your success, it's much harder for it to be taken away. Likewise, the education and skill set you develop for yourself, along with the positive mindset and the attitude you adopt can't ever be taken away.

The easiest way to move ahead in any industry and with any employer is to position yourself as someone who easily fits into the established work culture. Being able to meet the responsibilities of your job is important, but fitting in based on how you dress and how you act is equally important.

For example, consider someone who has recently graduated from the top of their class at a prestigious Ivy League school. This person has a degree in literature and edited her school's literary journal; she hopes to pursue a job working for a traditional publishing company. She's totally qualified for the job from a skills and knowledge standpoint, but her fashion sense leaves something to be desired. She has bright blue colored highlights in her hair, multiple piercings, and a wardrobe that makes her look like a punk rocker. This virtually guarantees she won't get hired, even though from a knowledge and skills (qualifications) standpoint, she's perfect for the job.

Employers hate taking risks when it comes to hiring employees. Companies want to hire people they are confident will fit perfectly into the company's culture, who will work hard, and who will be a team player. Even though some companies say they're looking for creative thinkers, these companies are still looking for people who will conform to the established policies and practices.

Part of being able to achieve your professional goals involves knowing what type of job you're looking to fill, what you're qualified for, and then positioning and marketing yourself in a way that will attract an employer's attention. While you always want to be totally honest with a potential employer, you also want to look and dress the part as you participate in the job search and job interview process. As you meet potential employers, it's important to dress like you already have the job.

Dressing the part doesn't necessarily mean going out and spending a fortune on designer clothes. It means shopping smart and dressing in a style that's appropriate for your line of work. Starting with the first time you meet a potential employer face-to-face in a job interview situation, you want your outward appearance to be consistent with what's normal within the company and industry in which you hope to work.

WALK THE WALK AND TALK THE TALK

In addition to what you wear, how you style your hair, what accessories you utilize (such as a briefcase), your attitude, your style of communication, and how you carry yourself will all contribute to the conclusions people make about you. Your body language and facial expressions, how physically fit you are, and how you handle yourself in various situations, along with what you actually say and do will all impact your professional image and reputation, plus contribute to someone's all important first impressions of you.

Just having the core qualifications necessary to meet the responsibilities of any job is important, but it's not enough. You'll always need to dress and act like someone who is qualified, confident, friendly, hard working, and success-oriented. While you always want to be looking out for your own interests, the perception you want others to have about you is that you care for the well-being of others, you're a team player, and you're dedicated to participating in a team effort in order to achieve your employer's goals.

There's a fine line between being a free thinker (and someone who is able to work and achieve success) and someone who is perceived as a troublemaker or rebel at work. While you want to fit in within the environment you work in, you never want to give up your personal or professional goals or identity in order to become a conformist or corporate drone. Choosing to work in an environment that is well-suited to your values and tastes will help diminish any conflict between being yourself and fitting into your work environment.

As you embark on a new job search, pay attention to what other people wear, their attitude, and their overall appearance. While it's totally acceptable to dress according to your own tastes, this must be kept under control and within what's considered the norm. Using make-up, accessories, or fashion to make a strong personal statement or stand out from the crowd can easily backfire and have a negative impact on how you're perceived by others. Make-up, your hairstyle, accessories, and the clothes you wear should be used to covey the proper image for the job you're in (or hope to fill), but at the same time, can convey your own personal taste if this is done subtly.

While you never want to "sell out," you should walk the walk and talk the talk that's appropriate for the field you're in (or hope to break into).

WARDROBE AND ACCESSORIES

When it comes to buying a new wardrobe, pay attention to the difference between fads and trends. A trend is something that stays around for more than one season. Spend your money on key articles of clothing. Refrain from taking your fashion cues from fashion magazines. Instead, pay attention to fashion catalogs, ads, and in-store displays. Wearing designer clothing is not a prerequisite for looking good. If you're going to buy a designer suit, that's fine, but you can then buy non-designer shirts to go with it. Men and women can use shirts as an accessory to modify outfits. A men's blazer can be worn with an oxford shirt for one look and a mock turtleneck for a totally different look, for example.

Spend your money on the key wardrobe pieces, like skirts, pants, jackets, suits, and dresses. Purchasing a nice coat, such as an overcoat, is always a good investment for men and women, because it's a timeless article of clothing from a fashion standpoint. You'll often meet people for the first time when you're still wearing your coat. Owning and wearing a nice trench coat (that's stylish and fits well), for example, will always help you make a positive first impression.

Anyone can redo their entire professional wardrobe for between $1,000 and $3,000, and it will last for several years if you buy key pieces that are of good quality. You can then maintain your wardrobe by spending just a few hundred dollars in subsequent years in order to add new shoes and accessories, for example.

Shopping for a new wardrobe doesn't mean you have to spend a fortune in order to be stylish. Watch for sales, shop at discount retailers, visit outlet stores, and don't forget about vintage clothing shops. Before wearing a new outfit in public, preview it in the privacy of your home. Try on your new outfit along with all of the accessories you plan to wear with it. Check to see that shades and textures match, and that the sleeves and hems are the correct length.

Finally, when investing in a new wardrobe, never skimp on alterations. There is no substitute for a good fit. Spending a fortune on a business suit is worthless unless it fits properly and enhances your image. Form a good relationship with your tailor and dry cleaner in order to help ensure that your clothes will last longer, look better, and fit you properly.

Once the key clothing elements of your wardrobe are in place, add accessories, such as jewelry, to enhance the look or change it over time. Men can use ties, their wristwatch, belts, shoes, the pens they carry, their briefcase, and other accessories to add to their overall look. Women can use jewelry, scarves, purses, shoes, and their hairstyle to alter or improve their overall look.

Make sure the colors, styles, and overall image is consistent with what's standard within your industry or at the company for which you work. When you begin a new job, for example, before investing a fortune in a new wardrobe, spend a few days watching what others you work with are wearing. Get an idea for styles, color schemes and the types of clothing that's appropriate, then find a way to bring your own personal taste into the mix as you expand your professional wardrobe.

. . . .

Not everyone has good fashion sense. If you believe what you wear may be hurting your image, consider hiring an image consultant to assist in compiling your professional wardrobe. A fashion or image consultant can help you define your image, better organize your existing wardrobe to create more coordinated outfits, and help you shop for articles of clothing that will enhance your overall image.

An example of an image consultant who works with business professionals is Mary Lou Andre, the founder and president of Needham, Massachusetts-based Organization By Design (781-444-0140/www.dressingwell.com). This is a wardrobe management and fashion consulting firm that helps individuals and organizations understand the power of being appropriately dressed in a variety of situations.

YOUR ATTITUDE AND PERSONALITY

If you want to someday become the senior vice president of marketing at your company, there's no reason why you can't start working toward that objective right now by obtaining the additional training, education, skills, and experience that will be required to make you qualified for the position. Likewise, there's no reason why you can't begin dressing the part in order to showcase yourself as someone who is professional, motivated, and success oriented.

Another major piece in the formula for success is your overall attitude and personality. Are you cheerful, friendly, outgoing, easy to talk to, a good listener, and generally someone other people enjoy working with and being around? Do people respect you, look up to you, and make an effort to spend time with you? Are you perceived by your employer as someone who is dedicated, loyal, hard working, and willing to work with others?

If you're truly passionate about the work you do, this will be readily apparent in your overall attitude and show through in your personality. Likewise, if you're constantly stressed out, in a bad mood, and/or you hate your work (and those you work with), this too will become apparent to those around you.

As you begin to formulate your professional self and discover who you are, what your goals are, and why you're trying to accomplish your professional goals, consider your own attitude and personality. Make sure you're being perceived positively by those around you. If you have concerns that the image you're conveying isn't what it should be, or your personality needs to be improved upon, these are things that should be addressed immediately.

Having a positive attitude and friendly personality isn't something that can necessarily be taught. However, it's typically a mindset that can be consciously adopted. If you're miserable in your current job, for example, this will have a long-term negative impact on your attitude and personality. It's virtually impossible to remain excited and happy about something that you truly dislike. If you alter your work situation so it begins to be closer to what makes you motivated, your overall attitude will slowly change for the better. This will happen subconsciously and automatically, once you make the conscious decision you want changes to happen and then begin taking steps to make these changes possible.

While it's important to maintain a positive attitude and upbeat (and friendly) personality for your own well being and success, this will also greatly impact how others perceive you. Your employer, for example, will be much more apt to promote someone who is perceived to be likable and hard working, as opposed to someone who is difficult to work with, who always watches the clock, and who doesn't work well with others.

YOUR DAY-TO-DAY BEHAVIOR

When you wake up each morning, are you excited to get out of bed, dress in an outfit that helps you convey an image you're proud of, and then go to work with a passion for achieving success? Realistically, it's virtually impossible to maintain this level of positive attitude every single day, but are the majority of your days filled with happiness?

At the end of each day, are you proud of what you've achieved and who you are as a person, or are you ashamed of the actions you took, how you treated others, and generally disappointed in the direction your professional life seems to be heading? On a day-to-day basis, the actions you take and the small, seemingly mundane decisions you make can have a tremendous impact on you and those around you.

Virtually everyday you're going to be confronted with decisions. You might be given the opportunity to take credit for someone else's work, stab a coworker in the back in order to move your career forward, steal supplies from your employer, or do something that might be considered unethical (but that will potentially benefit you personally). Whether or not you give in to these temptations will impact who you become as a person and how others perceive you.

As you make decisions and take actions on a day to day basis, no matter how insignificant the situation may seem, think about the short- and long-term repercussions of your actions and decisions. Will the decision(s) you make or the action(s) you take help you eventually achieve your long-term goals? How will you benefit? What will be the positive and negative impact on others and on your career?

Once you adopt a professional image and start building up your professional reputation, it's necessary to maintain it. Even the slightest deviation could have negative repercussions, especially when you're dealing with how others perceive you and what others think of you. If you want to be known as someone who is honest, caring, friendly, and ethical, this is how you must always act, each and every day. These aren't qualities you can adopt only when it's convenient.

MAKING YOURSELF STAND OUT FROM THE CROWD

Especially if you're working for a large company or you're one of dozens (if not hundreds) of people applying for a single job opening, it's very easy to get lost in the crowd. If you're hoping to land a job, earn a promotion or raise, or take on more responsibilities at work, it's important that you stand out from the crowd in a positive way. There are many ways of doing this, but one of the most effective is to showcase a positive and upbeat attitude as well as a pride and confidence in yourself.

Your attitude, appearance, hairstyle, body language, and personality can all be used to help you stand out from the crowd in a positive way. It's your responsibility, however, to create a positive image for yourself and then work hard to maintain it. At the same time, make sure you don't work too hard to create and maintain your image to the point where you're looked upon as being conceited, self-centered, or egotistical.

Always remember that the reputation you develop for yourself over time will stick with you throughout your career. While it's all too easy to destroy a good reputation quickly, it's far more difficult (and sometimes close to impossible) to fix a badly tarnished reputation, especially if you work in a close-knit company or industry where everyone knows one another. If you have developed a negative image, it will most likely follow you from job to job unless you take aggressive steps to begin repairing it.

If you believe you've somehow tarnished your reputation or image, determine exactly what you did and begin learning from your mistakes. Next, focus on what you can do, starting immediately, to begin repairing the damage you've done. This might mean making apologies to others, taking positive actions to counteract negative ones, or giving your personality a major overhaul for the better to ensure you become better liked among those around you.

USING YOUR RESUME AND COVER LETTER
TO MARKET YOURSELF

Obviously, the best way for someone to get to know you and develop an accurate perception of who you are is to meet you in-person and spend time with you. In a professional situation, when you're involved in the job search process, for example, this isn't always possible (at least initially). Most job search efforts begin when an job seeker submits a resume and cover letter as they apply for a job opening.

While a resume and cover letter are designed to help a potential employer get to know you, they are extremely impersonal. Your appearance and personality don't really come across on one or two sheets of paper that summarize your qualifications and accomplishments.

Nonetheless, in today's job market, your resume and cover letter become important job search tools. These are documents that must help you make a positive first impression, and in a matter of seconds (the amount of time a potential employer views your documents) must work as powerful marketing tools on your behalf. These documents must conform to standards, but at the same time, capture the reader's interest enough so that a potential employer decides he or she wants to meet you in person. At that point, you can use your personality and appearance to sell yourself as being the perfect applicant for the job.

Just as your personal appearance plays a major role as other people develop their perceptions of you and make their all-important first impression, the appearance and format of your resume and cover letter are as important as what these documents actually say about you. The book *Great Resume* (LearningExpress), which I also wrote, focuses specifically on how to create resumes and cover letters that will make a positive impact on the reader. The remaining portion of this chapter offers tips and strategies for using your resume and cover letter as powerful tools for marketing yourself.

Creating Your Resume So It Makes an Impact

For a job seeker, a resume is probably their most valuable job search tool. Typically, it will be the information contained on this single sheet of paper that determines whether or not you're invited for an interview and ultimately land the job for which you're applying.

Ideally, the information offered in your resume should be totally accurate, contain no spelling or grammatical errors, be easy to read and understand, and contain all of the important information an employer needs to know about you, the applicant. Knowing you'll have the attention of the person initially reading your resume for less than 30 seconds, the information you attempt to convey must be succinct.

Everything about the resume document itself, including the resume format you choose, the font the text is printed in, the style of your writing, the wording you use, and the actual content will be evaluated. Next to being dishonest and listing false or exaggerated information, the biggest mistake applicants make when creating a resume is including too much information or information not directly relevant to the job for which they're applying.

To keep your resume short (no longer than one side of one 8.5" by 11" page), it's critical to avoid adding irrelevant information. Likewise, if you're trying to pad your resume to make it longer, don't add fluff in order to compensate for a lack of work experience, for example.

Sue Nowacki is a professional resume writer and the president of 1st Impact Resume & Career Strategies, Inc. (904-794-5807, www. 1st-impact.com). "What the employer wants to read on a resume is information that is totally relevant and valuable to the position you're applying to fill. Everything else they simply don't care about," she said.

As you begin writing your resume, always be asking yourself if the information is directly relevant. Does the information make you appear more valuable to the employer and more qualified to fill the specific job you're applying for? If the information doesn't apply, don't include it. "The more clutter you add to your resume, the lower the chances of the important information actually being noticed and read," said Nowaski.

It's an excellent strategy to customize your resume for each job for which you apply. This can be done quickly and easily using specialized resume creation computer software, such as ResumeMaker Deluxe Edition ($39.95, Individual Software, 800-331-3313, www. individualsoftware.com), on a PC-based computer. While the software will help you format your resume and even choose the best wording for the information you choose to include, it's ultimately your responsibility to determine what information the employer wants and needs to see on your resume and to offer only that information.

To help determine what information about yourself is essential, think carefully about each specific job for which you're applying. What are the education, skills, and work experience requirements the employer will be looking for as they attempt to fill the position?

What specific information can you provide in order to showcase your qualifications?

"As you list your previous work experience and the responsibilities you had in each of your previous jobs, you also want to list major achievements in order to give the reader a sense you were good at your past jobs. Thus, you want to highlight specific achievements as well as the benefits and value you offered to past employers," said Nowaski.

The portion of your resume that lists your employment history might have the heading "Employment," "Work Experience," "Job History," "Professional Experience," or "Employers." The information in this section of your resume should list each employer, your job title, dates of employment, the city and state of the employer, one or two well-written sentences about your key responsibilities, and then three or four short sentences or bulleted items describing specific accomplishments.

Whenever possible, list quantitative data, such as "Managed over 200 accounts generating $1 million in annual sales," "Developed 41 new accounts in 18 months," or "Achieved a 24% average increase in sales over an 11-month period." These statements demonstrate achievements and value to a potential employer. If a bulleted item or descriptive sentence doesn't showcase your responsibilities and demonstrate positive results, don't include it.

Never list personal information on your resume that's not directly related to the job for which you're applying. Avoid listing hobbies. Also, refrain from including personal information the employer can't legally ask, such as your marital status, whether or not you have children, or your religion. "I recommend applicants list affiliations with professional associations when the information relates to the job. I recently worked with a client who wanted to list his 15-year membership in the Boy Scouts on his resume. This had nothing to do with the job he was applying for, so it was removed," said Nowaski.

While it's common for people to add a section to their resume listing awards and accolades, Nowaski believes this information should be included, when applicable, in conjunction with specific employment information, not in a separate section of the resume.

Thus, if you've been named Employee of the Month for six months in a row while working for the ABC Company, this piece of information should be included under the "Employment" section of your resume where you list the ABC Company.

If you're still employed, but searching for a new job, refrain from listing your current work phone number, fax number, and/or e-mail address at work on your resume unless you're comfortable with your current employer knowing about your job search efforts.

Finally, there's no need to include a line at the bottom of your resume stating, "References available upon request." This is assumed. If, however, you have specific and highly marketable skills, be sure they're clearly listed. As you write, edit, and proofread your resume, make an effort to keep all of the information short, to the point and totally relevant. Remember, any less important information can be discussed during a job interview. The purpose of your resume is to get an employer interested enough in you so you get invited for an interview. There's no need to convey your entire life's story using just your resume.

Making Your Resume Look Good

As a job applicant, when it comes to creating your resume and cover letter, how these documents look is as important as what they say. When applying for most jobs, you want your cover letter and resume to covey a highly professional and somewhat conservative image. To achieve this, you'll have to choose the right paper, select the right resume format, and decide whether or not to add a touch of color in order to make your resume stand out. Those resumes that stand out in a positive way will be the ones that the Human Resources department read first.

When you visit an office supply store or print shop to purchase resume paper, you'll be surprised at how many different shades of white there are to choose from. You can also find paper stocks in several different weights. Some will contain watermarks, and most will have at least some cotton content.

Paper Direct is a mail order paper company that offers a complete line of resume papers, as well as a large selection of more traditional paper stocks for use with resumes and cover letters. The company also offers a resume printing service. According to Linda Ireland, director of marketing at Paper Direct, "Choosing paper for your resume and cover letters is a personal decision; however, you want a paper with a high cotton content, and with a bond weight of 24 or 28 pounds. Watermarks aren't too important, but they do add to the overall high-quality image you're trying to convey."

As for resume paper color, the most traditional choices are bright white, ultra white, or ivory. It's also acceptable to use slate or light gray colored paper. Avoid using any bright-colored papers, which will cause your resume to stand out, but for the wrong reasons. Expect to pay between $.25 and $1.00 per sheet of quality resume paper.

"Paper Direct's resume paper packs contain paper for resumes, cover letters, and thank you notes, along with matching envelopes. Our designer papers will help an applicant's resume stand out in a positive way," said Ireland.

The ink color you choose for your resume and cover letters should be standard black; however, navy or burgundy ink can also be acceptable. Make sure the paper color and ink color work together to maximize readability. Some people choose to use a small amount of colored text within their resume to highlight specific items. This strategy can be effective; however, using multiple color inks is not considered traditional. Multicolor printing is also more expensive.

"You want your resume to stand out, but you also want your documents to look professional, and sometimes that's a contradiction. No matter what type of paper and color ink you select, it's vital that your resume, cover letters, thank you notes and envelopes all match. Part of being professional is being coordinated," said Ireland.

The type of job you're pursuing could also impact the look of your resume. Someone applying for a job as an accountant, for example, should definitely stick with a traditional white paper and black ink. A graphic artist, on the other hand, should show more creativity through the use of color.

When choosing resume paper, make sure you see and feel an actual sample of the paper stock, prior to purchasing a sealed package of that paper. Finally, if you'll be printing your resumes and cover letters on a laser or high-quality ink-jet printer, make sure the paper you choose was designed for this. Resume paper can be purchased from office supply stores, local print shops, and from specialty companies, like Paper Direct (800-272-7377/www.paperdirect.com).

Once your resume is written in a way that accurately represents who you are and conveys that information in a format and style you're proud of, make sure your cover letter complements your resume. This means the content in your cover letter should expand upon what's in your resume, and should visually look similar (using the same paper, font, and typestyles).

What you say in your resume and cover letter should prepare the reader for what they can expect from you once they meet you in person. These documents should be an accurate preview of who you are and what you can offer as an employee. Ultimately, these documents, like your overall image, should help you to pursue your long-term career goals.

SUCCESS STORY:
Will Develops His Professional Image and Markets Himself

WILL, A RECENT college grad, was having a run of bad luck in his job search. He was looking for an entry-level position in investment banking. He had good leads for a number of jobs, but his resume wasn't getting him called for interviews. Will examined his resume and the cover letters he was sending to see why his message wasn't getting across.

Will didn't have a lot of work experience but he knew that he had the skills to handle an entry-level position. He analyzed his strengths and looked for examples of achievements that exhibited what he considered to be his most important qualities: leadership, strong work ethic, interest in economics, and initiative. When Will revised his resume to emphasize his skills he found that he had more to add.

For example, his old resume listed that he was president of his fraternity for two years along with his other academic awards in his "Education" section. He decided to highlight this experience more effectively. A more complete description of his experience as his fraternity's president gave him an opportunity to quantify his leadership abilities and his initiative. During his presidency, he created Home Coming House Day, a house repairs day for alumni and new brothers followed with a big party. This innovative program increased alumni donations to the house by 35% and reduced the annual repairs bills by 50%. During his tenure the number of students pledging the house increased by 30%. By quantifying his successes, Will transformed a note on his resume into a powerful statement about his leadership and initiative.

Will also recast his description of his work-study job as a section leader for Economics 101. When he first wrote his resume, he assumed this teaching experience would be irrelevant to investment banking employers. However, he realized that his success as a section leader demonstrated his affinity for the subject, which he thought would be important to a financial employer. He also quantified his success; his resume now pointed out that his section was the most requested of all sections and the average grade on the final for the students in his section was 10 points higher than the class average. In his cover letter, Will emphasized how his skill set met the requirements of an entry-level position in investment banking. Will was soon called for several interviews and was even offered two positions in the same week. He chose the position that he thought offered him the best chance for advancement and is now enjoying his work at a top financial institution.

C H A P T E R 9

choosing a mentor

AS A CHILD, did you idolize a particular sports hero, musician, or celebrity? Did you dress like that person, try to emulate them in every way possible, and learn as much as you possibly could about their personal and/or professional life? Earlier in your life, did you consider pursuing a dream occupation, such as being a police officer, fireman, racecar driver, superhero, or circus performer, because that type of job seemed really cool at the time? Did you dress up in the appropriate uniform for the job when you played make-believe?

Young people often adopt role models or people to idolize based on how famous they are or how exciting their career seems to be. This is a perfectly normal part of growing up. As most of us get older, however, we tend to adopt a more independent philosophy and determine that we can figure things out on our own. We often begin to ignore advice from parents and elders, and often don't focus on choosing mentors or role models to help us succeed in our professional lives.

There are many lessons that can be learned from role models and mentors, no matter how old you are or what profession you have chosen to pursue. How you benefit from adopting a role model or mentor, however, will depend on whom you choose and what your relationship is to that person. Even if you're a highly educated adult with a respectable job, there's nothing embarrassing or unusual about adopting a role model or mentor. Once you learn how to utilize this type of person in your life, you'll probably discover many benefits.

This chapter explores the role a mentor or role model can play in your professional life (although they can be beneficial in your personal life as well) and discusses some of the ways you can enrich yourself by inviting this type of person into your life.

WHAT IS A MENTOR OR ROLE MODEL?

A role model or mentor is someone who is perhaps older, wiser and/or who has more experience. If the mentor or role model you choose is someone you know and have access to, this person can:

- Provide you with career-related support and encouragement
- Provide advice
- Teach you valuable skills
- Act as your advocate
- Make introductions on your behalf (help you network)
- Help you to make intelligent career-related decisions

You can choose role models whom you don't know and to whom you have no direct access. They might include a high-profile business leader, historical figure, sports hero, or a celebrity. In this situation, what you learn from the person you choose as a role model will probably come from research. As you learn about the person, you can choose what qualities you most admire and then adopt or emulate them. By discovering what the person you look up to did to become successful, for example, you can learn from their accomplishments (and mistakes) and potentially follow in their footsteps.

Why reinvent the wheel? If someone else has already discovered a formula for success in your industry, for example, why not learn from what they've done as opposed to spending the time and energy trying to figure out for yourself what someone else already knows.

The idea behind a role model or mentor isn't to copy exactly what they've done and to become a clone of that person. Instead, you want to study what made the person you admire successful and/or focus on specific qualities you like about that person and learn as much as possible from them.

You can obviously never meet or speak with former President John F. Kennedy, for example, but you can read all about him, watch documentaries about him, and learn about his philosophies and accomplishments. You can than adopt some of his personal qualities based upon what you learn. You can then use this acquired knowledge to help you become successful in whatever it is you set out to achieve.

Perhaps you admire the way the former president spoke in public or how he dealt with others. You might not agree with his political philosophies or with his personal actions outside of office, but you can learn from studying various aspects of his political career and success.

Michael Eisner, president and CEO of The Walt Disney Company, is one of the most powerful people in the entertainment industry and business world. Most people will never actually get to meet with or work directly with Eisner, but he is one of the most respected business leaders in America and someone who many people look up to as a role model. So much has been written about Eisner's unique management philosophies and business practices that it's possible for someone to do research and adopt some of his practices into their own management style, for example.

A role model and mentor serve the same basic purpose, but can be defined a bit differently. A role model can be someone whom you might never get to meet or work directly with, but whom you can learn from, such as a celebrity, high profile business leader, or historical figure. A mentor, however, is someone who you know, have access to, and can potentially work with one-on-one.

A mentor typically involves having a learning relationship between you and someone who you believe can disseminate knowledge, insight, advice, and support. The relationship should be based upon mutual respect, and trust. Whom you choose as a role model and/or mentor is a very personal decision and one that's based on whom you respect and believe you can learn from.

Yes, it's possible to have both role models and mentors in your professional life, just as it's possible to have several role models but no mentors or vice versa. It's important to understand, however, that a mentor or role model should not become someone whom you overly rely on to make all of your important decisions. The purpose of a role model or mentor is not to adopt a surrogate parent or boss—it's to offer you support, encouragement, motivation and guidance as you make your own career-related decisions and pursue your own professional goals and ambitions.

CHOOSING A MENTOR OR ROLE MODEL

The person you choose to adopt as your role model or mentor can be virtually anyone whom you respect and from whom you believe you can learn something. Remember, as you select this person, you're looking to obtain new knowledge or emulate some aspect of that person's success. You're not trying to actually become that person. Throughout your personal and professional life, you will evolve and your mentoring needs will change. Thus, whom you look to for advice or guidance right now may change in the future.

As you think about who a good role model or mentor might be for you, ask yourself questions like:

- What is it about a particular person that interests you?
- What has he or she achieved that you admire?

- What personal qualities does the person posses that you'd like to adopt?
- What specifically do you think you'll be able to learn from the person?
- How much access (if any) can you have to the potential mentor or role model?
- How can you best utilize your time spent with your mentor?
- How can you learn more about the potential role model?
- What do you want to know?

The following is a list of some potential people you might consider adopting as a role model or mentor.

- Boss—This is typically someone who has achieved a greater level of professional success than you. He or she has worked hard and has acquired the skills, experience, and know-how to be an effective leader. By studying this person, perhaps you can learn what steps they followed in their own career path to reach their current level of success. The benefit of having a boss who is also your mentor is that this person can open up doors for you, create opportunities, teach you skills, and provide you with knowledge that will be beneficial to your specific job at your company and in your industry.
- Business Leader/Industry Leader—Perhaps you have (or someday will) read a profile or interview with a business leader in a publication such as *The Wall Street Journal, Forbes, Inc., Fast Company,* or *BusinessWeek.* As you read the article (or hear the person speak at a trade show, or see them on television, for example), something about the person catches your attention. Maybe you'll obtain a valuable piece of advice or develop a tremendous level of respect for that person as you learn how they overcame difficult obstacles to achieve their success. You may never meet the person you read about in person or have a chance to speak with them on the phone, but you can do research to learn more about them and learn from their experiences. No matter what you do for

a living, there's always something useful you can learn from someone else who has achieved a high level of success, whether or not that person works in your industry.

- Coworker—Someone who you work with (or previously worked with) can be a wonderful source of ongoing encouragement and guidance as you participate in the day-to-day trials and tribulations associates with your job. Your coworker(s) will be able to understand what you're going through professionally, because they're currently having similar experiences.

- Entertainer—Whether it's a TV star, movie star, or recording artist, people often idolize famous people. You may look to famous people for fashion and hairstyle tips, for example. Or you might truly respect an entertainer because of something in particular he or she has accomplished. Maybe it's the charity work they do that attracts your attention. Maybe you appreciate his or her sense of humor or want to adopt aspects of their personality to make yourself more socially successful. If you choose to adopt a celebrity as your role model, keep in mind, the public image of the celebrity may have been created by a manager and/or publicist, and it may be very different from who these people actually are as individuals.

- Friend—A close friend is someone you can trust, who will always watch your back, provide you with honest criticism and feedback, and who will be a source of endless love and support. Like a marriage or any personal relationship, a friendship should be based on honesty. If there's something you particularly respect about a friend, perhaps you can learn from them and ultimately become a better person. Perhaps your friend can be the foundation for your personal support system or someone who can offer you the guidance you need to make important decisions.

- Historical Figure—Someone famous from history (whether they're living or dead) can be a positive role model, especially if you're interested in learning how and why the person became successful, overcame obstacles and achieved the success they did. Through research, a lot can be learned from and about historical figures. This knowledge can be applied to help you make important career-related decisions.

- Parent or Relative—Many people look to their parents as a source of support and encouragement. Often, parents are more than willing to provide advice and guidance (even when it's not requested). Parents often have a deep commitment to helping their children find success. Because of the pressure a parent is often capable of putting on their child (you), it's important to discover how to accept a parent's advice, without being pushed into decisions they make for you. However, a parent's commitment to your success combined with their accumulated life experience and their insight into your character often give parents a unique ability to serve as a mentor. Just as parents can be excellent role models, so can brothers, sisters, and other close relatives whom you admire.

- Politician—Just as a lot can be learned from successful business leaders, the same is true of some politicians. There are (and have been) many politicians worthy of being role models. From these people, a lot can be learned about leadership, decision-making, and public speaking, for example.

- Religious Leader—Many people look to their religion for guidance with personal and/or professional issues, and a religious leader can often provide the comfort, guidance, and support one needs to face difficult challenges in their life.

- Schoolmate—Just as friends can be excellent mentors, so can people who went (or go to) school with you. These are your peers—people with a similar educational background, who might excel in different areas than you, but still share common ideas and/or values. While your educational experience is shared with a schoolmate, chances are your personal backgrounds will be different, as will your professional aspirations. This can provide you with an opportunity to share ideas and learn from the experience of others.

- Sports Hero—One thing that most (if not all) professional athletes and sports heroes share is their driving desire to succeed in whatever highly competitive sport they participate it. Someone who plays for the NBA, WNBA, NFL, MLB, PGA, LPGA, or NFL, for example, who competes on an Olympic team, or who becomes a top-ranked NASCAR driver, is among the best in the world at his or her sport. These people have figured out how to transform their passion for a sport into a lucrative living, and they continue to push themselves toward perfecting their skill and ability to compete and win. This drive for success, the need to always be practicing one's craft, and the ability to outsmart or outplay the competition are skills that can be adopted by people from all walks of life and incorporated into one's daily life. Sports heroes are highly motivated and have an internal desire to win and be the best that they can, despite whatever challenges they face. These too are qualities from which everyone can benefit. By studying a particular athlete, learning about them and discovering what makes him or her successful, you too can benefit from what the athlete has mastered.
- Teacher/Professor—We look to teachers and professors to educate us on specific topics or subjects, however, many educators have a wide range of experiences and knowledge that they can impart on those with the desire to learn. Teachers and professors are often considered experts in their field and can thus offer guidance for someone interested in pursuing a career in a specific area. For example, if your professional goal is to become a lawyer, adopting a professor from your law school as a mentor can be extremely educational and beneficial to your career. Chances are, your mentor in this situation will be able to help guide you to become the best lawyer possible and make introductions for you, and help you network upon graduation. He or she might also be able to help you down the road as you prepare for difficult cases or face professional challenges that require the guidance from someone who is older and with more experience.

WHAT YOU CAN LEARN FROM YOUR MENTOR

If you're lucky enough to have a mentor with whom you have direct and ongoing access, what you can learn from this person is limited only by the knowledge and experience the mentor possesses. Once you begin to cultivate a personal and professional relationship with a mentor, it's important to allow that relationship to grow over time. Without making unrealistic demands on the person, you'll want to learn as much as possible from them and take advantage of whatever opportunities he or she can help create for you.

The expectations you have of your mentor, however, should be realistic. You'll probably discover that the relationship you develop with your mentor (and the fact that you adopt a specific person as your mentor) will happen over time and probably won't be a premeditated series of events. Once you pinpoint someone you'd like as your mentor, and you begin seeking guidance from him or her, maintain an open mind regarding the advice that's offered. While the person you look up to may be extremely experienced and knowledgeable, the advice or guidance he or she offers isn't gospel. You should always remain free to make your own decisions and pursue your own destiny.

FOLLOWING IN YOUR MENTOR'S FOOTSTEPS

A role model or mentor is someone you can learn from. It's someone who can help you expand your knowledge and who can help create opportunities for you. Your mentor, for example, can help you build up your network of professional contacts, make introductions for you when seeking a job, help you make important decisions, and share his or her first-hand experience.

In some cases, it's very appropriate to want to follow directly in the footsteps of your mentor or role model in order to reach a similar level of success. As you do this, however, you want to maintain your own personal and professional identity, yet borrow from the mentor or role model the skills, knowledge, or qualities you most admire.

UTILIZING MULTIPLE MENTORS

When it comes to learning from others, there is no limit to the number of people you can adopt as role models or mentors. For example, you may believe someone like Anthony Robbins is the perfect role model when it comes to perfecting your public speaking abilities and/or pursuing your quest to become a happier, more motivated, and better-organized person. You might not want to become a motivational speaker yourself, but you might want to adopt some of his talent for truly inspiring others.

At the same time, you might look to another business leader in order to learn how they expertly manage people or have overcome professional challenges that you are currently facing. What's important to understand is that it's an excellent strategy to adopt role models and mentors who will inspire you, help you achieve success, and who can assist you in overcoming your specific weaknesses. As you begin to work toward achieving your personal, professional, and financial goals, you'll want to learn from as many people as possible in order to achieve your own success. After all, there's probably no reason why the formula someone else used to achieve his or her success won't also work for you. What you need to do is study how and why an individual achieved his or her success or overcame his or her obstacles, then figure out how you can do something similar.

When you have direct access to you mentor, use your time with that person to ask plenty of questions. Utilize the time you spend with your mentor as a valuable learning experience.

Once you've set your own personal and professional goals, actively seek out role models and mentors whom you believe can assist you on your quest to achieve your goals. Look to experts in your field for knowledge, people you know and care about for support, and anyone else whom you believe has qualities you greatly admire.

YOU TOO CAN BECOME A MENTOR

At some point in your professional life, you too may have the opportunity to become a mentor or role model for someone younger and/or less experienced than you. Once you've achieved some level of success, why not use what you've learned to help others? Becoming a mentor or role model for someone can be a tremendously rewarding experience.

SUCCESS STORY:
Emma Finds a Mentor

EMMA HAD BEEN at her new job as senior product manager at a large media firm for about a month. She was having some difficulty adjusting to a large, corporate office after five years in a relatively small department of a medium-sized PR firm. This cultural change, coupled with the fact that she reported to an off-site, "hands-off" manager with dotted lines all over the organization, often left her without any direct advisement or supervision.

Late one evening, Emma was struggling to make sense out of an assignment to work with a certain outside agency on an upcoming project. In going through some old files, she came across a memo related to this outside agency that was written by Magda, a senior vice president of another division. Magda's office was just down the hall. Often, Emma passed this woman's door on the way out of the building at night, noting that Magda was a fellow late-night worker on an otherwise empty hall. Emma decided to pop in, introduce herself, and ask for some background information regarding the outside agency.

As it turned out, Magda used to work in Emma's division, and not only understood that division's office politics, but she was also working with the same outside agency. Magda proved to be a very knowledgeable resource, and she seemed genuinely interested in Emma and her project. Following this introduction, Magda would forward relevant industry news items to Emma's attention or periodically check in with her on her way to grab a cup of coffee. Emma immediately realized that a high-profile corporate ally was a real asset in this business, while also noting that Magda was clearly interested in her personal success, and her career with the firm.

Emma was proactive; she recognized a good mentoring opportunity when it was offered. She happened upon a successful executive looking for a means to help a talented individual on the rise. She read corporate reorganization memos, took note of the people behind the nameplates, and paid attention to those working in the world around her. She was also careful to choose a mentor who was not directly a part of her division, but still within her field.

Before submitting her project proposal, Emma approached Magda with the document for her feedback. Magda provided the constructive critique that Emma needed, along with the corporate-specific protocol that Emma couldn't have known as a new hire. The result was an approved product plan for Emma and a valuable career mentor, too.

developing your network

GETTING AHEAD IN the business world isn't just a matter of what you know, how hard you work, how educated you are, or what skills you possess. It also involves who you know and how you utilize those contacts. Throughout your personal and professional life, you're going to encounter many people. Each one of these people has his or her own set of contacts, knowledge base, and skill set. Through networking, you can learn how to utilize the resources of other people.

Depending on the type of work you do, chances are achieving success will somehow (directly or indirectly) involve the help of others—the people in your network. Bosses, coworkers, subordinates, clients, customers, friends, relatives, professors, professional acquaintances, personal acquaintances, and people you meet in your day to day life can all easily become part of your ever growing network.

TAPPING INTO YOUR NETWORK

When you decide to purchase an expensive product, such as a major appliance, a new car, or when you need to hire a lawyer, doctor, or contractor, for example, chances are you ask people you know for a referral. After all, you probably trust the recommendation of a friend, relative, or coworker as opposed to an ad in the Yellow Pages. Asking someone you know for a referral is just one basic example of networking—tapping the knowledge of others you know to obtain reliable information.

Networking can help you obtain new clients or customers, discover unadvertised job openings, obtain information, or create opportunities that wouldn't otherwise be open to you.

Just as you always want to be working toward achieving your long term personal, professional, and financial goals, you always want to be building up your network. This can be done in a variety of ways, all of which are extremely easy.

As you build up your network, you'll need to tap your social skills, interact with people, strike up conversations with strangers, and become a good listener. When you meet someone new, ask questions and make conversation in an effort to learn more about the person. Demonstrate a genuine interest in what the person has to say, and in the process of meeting new people, exchange business cards. You never know if the person you just met might someday become a valuable new customer or client, be able to provide a referral, or offer you some type of new opportunity.

There are many ways of meeting new people to expand upon your network. Begin with the people who are already your friends, coworkers, business associates, and relatives. To meet additional people who work in your industry, for example, consider attending trade shows and meetings sponsored by various professional organizations or associations.

Doing volunteer work, becoming an active member of your church or temple, attending events sponsored by your local Chamber of Commerce, getting involved in local or regional politics, or simply attending social events organized by friends all offer excellent opportunities for meeting new people.

Part of networking means being able to provide advice or referrals, in addition to seeking them out. As you expand your network, it's important to keep track of people. The best way to do this is to collect business cards and start a comprehensive database of contact information. (Tools for networking are addressed later in the chapter.) If, however, you're comfortable using a computer or a PDA (such as the Palm V), storing contact information using an electronic address book or contact management software package is an excellent idea. Maintaining a well-organized contact database will take some discipline and time on your part, but you'll find that over time, the benefits will far outweigh the few minutes it takes to enter the name, address, phone number, and related information for a new acquaintance into your database.

When you need information or have to track someone down with knowledge or skills in a specific area, for example, having a well-established network can be a great help. Likewise, if you're looking for a job in a specific industry or with a particular employer, one of the best ways to get your foot in the door is through a personal introduction. Even if you don't directly know someone who can help you, chances are someone in your network will know someone else who can. Making and obtaining referrals and utilizing the contacts of the people you already know is part of what effective networking is all about.

DEVELOPING YOUR NETWORKING SKILLS

How hard you work to constantly expand and utilize your network is entirely up to you. If you're comfortable meeting new people and holding conversations with them, you'll find that expanding your network can be easy and even fun. For example, if you're traveling alone on a business trip, strike up a conversation with the person sitting next to you on the airplane. If you belong to a health club, chat with the person working out on the treadmill next to yours. You never know when you'll come across someone you find interesting.

Many books, videos, and audio courses are available that can teach you how to improve upon your verbal communication skills and feel more comfortable holding conversations with strangers. Part of this involves having confidence in yourself, knowing what types of questions to ask, and becoming a good listener.

Chances are, when you meet someone new, that person feels just as awkward as you do when it comes to striking up an intelligent conversation. Initially, what you discuss is irrelevant. You can discuss the weather, current events, a movie or TV show you've seen, a book you've read, the outfit the person you've just met is wearing, your occupations, your family, or how a sports team is performing. The trick is to find what you and the other person have in common and then build upon those common areas of interest.

A major part of becoming someone who is skilled at networking involves learning how to be a good communicator. When you participate in conversations, convey to the other person that you're friendly, outgoing, honest, and interested in what they have to say. What you say, how you say it, and your body language (including your eye contact) during a conversation can all be used to convey the appropriate image and make you a better communicator.

TIPS FOR HOLDING A CONVERSATION

The following are some basic guidelines for holding a conversation with anyone, including a person you've just met and who has the potential of becoming part of your network.

- Listen to what the other person has to say. Never interrupt them in mid-sentence.
- Ask questions and follow-up questions. Develop a clear understanding of the person's ideas or philosophies.

- When appropriate, discuss your own opinions, ideas, and point of view. Refrain, however, from being argumentative.
- Make sure the level and tone of your voice is appropriate to the situation. If you speak too softly, you won't be heard. If you speak too loudly, you could be construed as arrogant or rude.
- Maintain a positive and polite attitude, even if the topic of conversation turns toward something in which you have no interest.
- As early in the conversation as possible, try to find common ground. For example, you may have mutual friends or acquaintances.
- People in general enjoy talking about themselves and their accomplishments. Most people are comfortable discussing themselves, so this topic should make striking up an initial conversation easier. At the same time, be sure to share interesting information about yourself.
- Use the other person's name often throughout the conversation.
- Maintain a good level of eye contact with the person you're speaking with.
- In terms of your body language, maintain a relaxed posture. Avoid fidgeting or doing something that makes you appear bored or uninterested in the conversation. Also, avoid entering into the other person's personal space.
- If you're having a conversation with someone you've just met, keep the topics of conversation upbeat and light. Don't delve into deeply personal or controversial issues.
- At the end of the conversation, end it politely. Say something like, "It was a pleasure meeting you." You might also want to exchange business cards, phone numbers, or e-mail addresses.

. . . .

It's important to always carry business cards in your wallet, pocket, briefcase, or purse. When a networking situation unexpectedly aris-

es, you should be prepared to exchange contact information in a professional manner. Also, always carry a pen so exchanging information with someone else who isn't carrying a business card will be easier.

....

TOOLS FOR NETWORKING

Aside from your own ability to communicate with others, make new friends, and convey a good level of confidence in yourself, there's not a whole lot you need to become effective at networking.

Once you start building up your network database, there are a handful of tools you can use to better organize this information and insure that it's readily available when you need it. These tools include:

- A personal organizer with address book. This is often a traditional paper binder, from a company such as Day-Timer, Inc., or Franklin Covey. In addition to maintaining your address book of personal and business contacts, these planners will also help you stay organized and manage your schedule.
- Business card file. Each time you collect a business card from a new contact, it should be filed so you'll easily be able to find it again in the future. If you maintain an electronic database of your contacts, your traditional business card file can be a backup. Whether you use a small index card file, a binder containing sheets of business card holders, or some other filing method, it doesn't matter, as long as you can find specific contact information when you need it.
- Contact management software, such as Act! 2000 (www.act.com) or Outlook 2000 (www.microsoft.com). These software packages integrate a powerful electronic address book with email, your word processor, database

management tools, and other functions. This allows you to quickly send an email, fax, or traditional letter, for example, to any of your contacts and maintain an ongoing record of your communications within your database. Thus, all information pertaining to a contact is linked together for easy reference and access. All information within a program, such as Act! 2000, for example, can be sorted or searched using any keyword, phrase, or criteria, so information is easy to find. These software packages also contain powerful schedule management capabilities.

- Personal digital assistant (PDA). These hand-held electronic devices, such as the Palm V (www.palm.com), have become incredibly powerful, yet easy-to-use tools for managing vast amounts of information. Using a PDA's built-in address book function, you can store names, addresses, phone numbers, fax numbers, mobile phone numbers, pager numbers, e-mail addresses, and other important information about all of your contacts. With a PDA, this information is available to you anywhere, anytime, not just when you're sitting at your computer.

To avoid confusion, it's always best to maintain a single database of personal and professional contacts. In a work environment, you should consider security issues when choosing a method for maintaining your database to insure your valuable information doesn't get copied or stolen. If you're using computer software, such as ACT! 2000 or a PDA, built-in password protection is available.

The people you enter into your database can be cross-referenced and sorted using a wide range of criteria, such as their first or last name, address, city, state, zip code, phone number, occupation, company name, or keyword.

While you might not remember the name of that insurance salesman you met at a cocktail party six months ago, for example, you might remember being impressed with him, so you can search your contact database based on the keyword "insurance" to find him. If you're now in the market for a new life insurance policy or a friend asks for a referral, you can easily track this person down in seconds because they're in your contact database.

These days, getting in touch with people can be a bit tricky, unless you're prepared to play a game of phone tag. As you gather information for your database, here are some basic guidelines regarding what specific information you might want to gather:

Name:_____

Title: _____

Company: _____

Work Address: _____

_____

_____

Work Phone: (____)_____Extension: _____

Home Phone: (____)_____

Cell Phone: (____)_____

Fax Number: (____)_____

Pager Number: (____)_____

E-mail Address: _____

Assistant/Secretary's Name: _____

Alternate Contact Name: _____

Spouse and Children's' Names (if applicable): _____

Home Address:_____

_____

Birth Date: ____/____/____

Occupation: _____

Notes:_____

_____

_____

_____

_____

_____

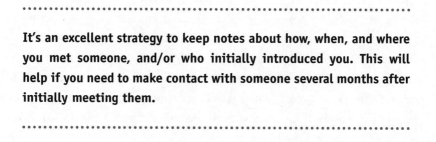

It's an excellent strategy to keep notes about how, when, and where you met someone, and/or who initially introduced you. This will help if you need to make contact with someone several months after initially meeting them.

BUSINESS CARD ETIQUETTE

Many business leaders will tell you that one of the keys to success in virtually any career is someone's ability to network. This means having the ability to meet new people, strike up conversations and then develop personal or professional friendships that can later somehow benefit you.

As you meet new people, whether it's through networking or in the course of meeting the responsibilities of your job, it's a common custom to exchange business cards.

Thanks to technological advancements during the past decade, most business professionals now have some, or all, of the following: a work phone number (with extension), fax number, pager number, cellular phone number, toll-free work number, e-mail address, a website, and a home telephone number.

Your business card can be a powerful marketing tool for you personally or your business. If you're already employed, your business card should focus on how a business acquaintance, client, customer, or someone interested in working with you or your company can contact you. Thus, you'll want to include your name, job title, company name, perhaps a one line description of what your company does, your company's website address, plus its mailing address, phone number, and fax number. Including your e-mail address on a business card is also common practice, since e-mail correspondence has become a primary way in which people communicate in corporate America.

Job seekers can also take advantage of business cards as a tool for marketing themselves. When you attend a job fair, send a resume to a company, or participate in a job interview, having personal business cards you can distribute to potential employers will help create a professional image and make it that much easier for someone to contact you. This type of business card contains only your personal contact information, not a company name or contact information for a current (or past) employer.

A personal business card should contain your name, address, home phone number, and/or your cellular number, and possibly an e-mail address. It should also contain one line describing your qualifications or what professional licenses or accreditations you possess.

Choosing to print a home telephone number on a business card is a decision that should be considered carefully. Do you really want people calling you at home in the evening or on weekends? Even if you're technically on-call with your clients, you're probably better off listing a cellular phone number or pager number someone can use if they need to reach you quickly. You can always hand-write your home telephone number on a business card for a specific client or customer if the situation warrants it.

The actual design and appearance of your business cards says a lot about you. It should look professional, be easy to read, and if possible, memorable. Using a graphic, such as a company logo or other visual elements, can make a business card more memorable.

Depending on your profession, different standards apply for what constitutes a professional looking business card. If you're a real estate agent or work in show business, for example, having your picture displayed on your business cards is appropriate. People who work as a graphic designer or artist might have extremely flashy-looking cards that use many colors and graphic images.

If you work in a more traditional occupation (for example, medicine, law, banking, or accounting), you'll probably want to stick with formal looking business cards that are printed using black or blue ink, that use a standard font, and that are printed on white card stock. Other than a corporate logo, avoid using fancy fonts or graphic elements. Your business cards should also match your company's letterhead (or your resume, if you're a job seeker) in terms of color and overall design.

Having standard black and white business cards printed, whether for personal or business use, is inexpensive. Adding multiple colors, unusual card stocks, photographs, or having the card printed in a different shape other than a standard rectangle will increase the printing costs.

Ordering business cards is as easy as visiting any print shop, such as Minuteman Press, CopyMax, Sir Speedy, CopyCop, or Kinko's, then choosing a layout and exact wording. Often, you'll be able to go through various design books and obtain the assistance of a graphic artist who will help you create professional-looking business cards.

While many different software packages allow you to design business cards on your computer, then print them out on a laser printer, the final result often looks unprofessional. By investing anywhere from $25.00 to $50.00 to have 1,000 business cards professionally printed (using raised print), the final result will look far more impressive.

Once you have your business cards printed, always carry some with you. Networking opportunities often arise when you least expect them. Being able to exchange business cards with people you meet will help enhance your base of network contacts and could lead to new business or job opportunities.

HOW, WHEN, AND WHERE TO NETWORK

Meeting new people and expanding your network is something that can be done virtually anytime, anywhere you happen to be. If you were to grab a pen and paper, chances are you could write down the names of at least 25 people who already exist in your network. These people might be family members, friends, coworkers, etc.

Some of the places where you can expand your network include:

- Attending local Chamber of Commerce meetings
- Attending parties or social gatherings hosted by friends, coworkers, or professional acquaintances

- Attending trade shows or conferences
- Attending evening or weekend classes (participating or teaching adult education programs)
- Becoming active in local politics. This will allow you to meet others in your town, city, state, or community
- Becoming active with your church, temple, or house of worship
- Contacting current, past, and potential customers or clients
- Contacting lawyers, accountants, and other business professionals who work with a handful of clients
- Attending events sponsored by your high school, college, or university alumni association
- Participating in industry association (or union) meetings or functions
- Using the Internet (newsgroups, chat rooms, bulletin boards, online conferences)
- Traveling on a business trip
- Volunteering or doing charity work
- Using your health club or golf club

UTILIZING YOUR NETWORK

Not only can you use network contacts to help you tap the unadvertised job market, you can also use it to find new customers or clients, gather information, seek out industry experts, or find people with specialized skills. Typically, when you tap the resources of your network, you want to treat your contacts with utmost respect, especially if you're asking for a favor.

Never make unrealistic requests or put someone out so much that they'll have no desire to help you (or regret helping you) later. Always thank the person for their help, both in person and with a follow-up thank you note, and offer your assistance should it be needed in the future.

When contacting someone in your network, assume that he or she is busy with their own personal and professional responsibilities.

Don't keep pestering someone by leaving multiple voice mail messages or sending multiple e-mail messages, for example. If you can't reach the person immediately by phone, try sending a single fax or e-mail message to follow up your voice mail message, then wait for the person to contact you.

If you don't know the person you're calling well, immediately refresh the person's memory in terms of how he or she knows you, where you met, or who introduced you. If someone told you to call a specific person in their network, immediately inform the stranger who gave you the referral and why. When you initially make contact, ask if the person is busy, or if they have a few minutes to speak with you. Again, you don't want to appear overbearing or demanding.

As you begin to utilize your network, you'll most likely find that people are willing to help others out if they're asked nicely. There will always be a handful of people who will want to know what's in it for them, but most people enjoy being able to help out others by utilizing their own experience, skills, knowledge, or contacts, assuming that offering the assistance doesn't overly tax the person's time or resources.

TIPS FOR A NETWORKING INTERVIEW

Sometimes arranging a formal informational interview with a networking contact can be extremely productive.

Whether you're meeting a new business contact for the first time or having a more formal meeting with someone you already know, the following tips will help you prepare for the experience and better utilize your networking and conversational skills.

1. Always dress professionally. This means no jeans, T-shirts, or sneakers. Remove nose rings, tongue piercings, and any other forms of personal expression that don't fit within the work environment of your contact. While rules about prefessional dress are much more flexible than they used to be, it's always

a good idea to err on the conservative side when you're meeting someone for the first time or attending a formal meeting. Use common sense to determine what will make a good impression.

2. Do research about the company for which your contact works, or the person you're about to meet for the first time. This will help you prepare intelligent questions to ask and develop a better understanding of what topics you need to cover during your conversation.

3. Create a list of questions you plan to ask during the informational interview. Since you've asked for the meeting it is very important that you come prepared with questions and that you don't expect your contact to carry the conversation.

4. Practice doing mock interviews with a friend or parent. Try posing your questions, and think about the questions your contact might ask you. Visualize yourself during the interview making a good impression.

5. Show up early for the interview or meeting. Whatever you do, don't be even one minute late. Allow for traffic and other unexpected delays.

6. Be polite to **everyone** you meet.

7. Never lie or stretch the truth about anything. Be open and honest about yourself, your skills, and your work experience. Your contact might recommend you for a job opening based on your interview, so his or her credibility will also be at stake.

8. Answer all questions posed to you in complete sentences, not just with a "yes" or "no" response. Ask plenty of well-thought-out questions about the person's career, the field you wish to enter, how you might further your career, and so on.

9. When you get home after the interview, immediately write and send a personalized thank you note to the person or people with whom you interviewed. Make reference to something

specific that you discussed during the interview to let your contact know that their advice was helpful. In a business meeting situation, exchange business cards and end the conversation by discussing how you'll proceed in the future in terms of your business relationship. If followup on your part is necessary, take the appropriate actions in a timely manner.

KEEPING IN TOUCH WITH YOUR NETWORK

Developing your network is an ongoing process. While meeting new people is important, you'll also want to maintain the personal and professional relationships you already have. The most important people in your network should receive your personal attention, however, to keep other relationships going, consider sending periodic personalized e-mail messages, notes, or other correspondence.

One of the best times to make contact with people on a personal level is around the holidays by sending Christmas, holiday, or New Year's cards. While this isn't as personal as an in-person meeting over lunch or dinner, for example, sending a card shows the person you're thinking about them and care about their friendship.

Having professional looking holiday cards printed is an option, but each card should contain a personalized, hand written message and be signed. If you're sending cards to business contacts, it's always a good idea to include your business card in the envelope.

Setting and achieving your personal and professional goals is something you'll ultimately need to do yourself. However, having a network in place can provide resources and support to make the process of achieving success much easier. The more people you know, and the more people who like you, respect you and consider you a friend, the better off you'll be, no matter what your career is.

SUCCESS STORY:
Juanita Creates a Network

JUANITA HAD JUST graduated from college with a degree in English Literature and Writing, and moved to New York City. She wasn't sure what sort of career she wanted to pursue. Throughout college she had worked as a teacher in various elementary age after-school programs; she really enjoyed working with children although she had already decided that she didn't want to be a teacher. Because she had a lot of childcare experience, and knew it was something she would enjoy doing for a little while, she decided to baby-sit for an agency while she decided what she really wanted to do. In addition, babysitting would provide Juanita with the opportunity to talk with many people working in many different fields.

Through her contact with various families around the city, Juanita learned about all sorts of different careers, and she began to build a network of people in various fields. Because she enjoyed reading, writing, and helping children so much, she decided after a couple of months that a job in educational publishing was the most appealing career choice. She began alerting her clients to the fact that she was in the market for an entry-level job at an educational publishing company. As luck would have it, one of the women for whom she babysat was in the marketing department at a small educational publishing company, which was also a budding e-learning website. Her client knew that the editorial department was looking for editorial assistants, so she recommended Juanita as a job candidate to the Vice President of Content at her company.

Not only did Juanita's experience working with school-aged children demonstrate to the VP that Juanita had a continuing interest in children, and elementary education, the VP also used the same agency to find sitters for her children. Thus, the VP knew the kind of people who worked for the agency. She knew that the woman who ran the agency had very high standards, and that all the agency sitters were reliable, caring, smart, and fun individuals, so she hired Juanita on the spot.

Because Juanita broadcast the message to her clients that she was conducting a job search, and also because she chose to include here agency-babysitting job on her resume, she was hired. Juanita learned that you never know which of your experiences people will react to; there is almost always a way to relate some of your experiences to the job for which you are applying so that they want to hire you on the spot!

CHAPTER 11

putting it all together

AS YOUR OWN career coach, your quest to reach your ultimate potential is about to begin. You now have the basic building blocks in place to plan your professional life and ultimately achieve your goals—if you're willing to complement the knowledge you posses with hard work, persistence, and dedication.

While you may be very entranced right now about achieving success, one of the biggest challenges you'll face from this point on is staying motivated as you're confronted with the challenges and obstacles that may get in your way as you begin implementing your action plans.

No matter what happens from this point forward, never lose focus of what you're trying to achieve and why you're trying to achieve it. If you can remain passionate about what you're trying to accomplish—whatever it may be—you'll find innovative ways of overcoming the challenges you face by tapping the various resources at your disposal. When your own resources aren't sufficient, you now know how to tap your network and/or obtain additional skills or knowledge.

When confronted by a problem or challenge, don't panic or lose your confidence. Focus on the problem or obstacle at hand, determine why it's a problem, and then figure out what specifically it will take to overcome it. Don't be afraid to use your own creativity or tap your network contacts for support or assistance. Make overcoming an obstacle your goal, develop an action plan for achieving the goal, then implement your action plan and lead yourself to success.

Hopefully as you've been reading this book, you've come to some realizations about yourself and your career, and have set goals that will help you ultimately achieve success and happiness in whatever you set out to do. Now, the trick is to remain focused as you begin putting in the time, energy, and hard work needed to transform your life.

By answering the following questions, you'll be able to summarize your goals and objectives, pinpoint the outcomes you're trying to achieve, and remind yourself why you've set the goals you have. You'll also focus on what achieving your intended outcomes means to you on a personal, professional, and financial level. Once you answer these questions, keep referring back to your answers so you'll better be able to stay focused and motivated over the long term.

GOAL SUMMARY WORKSHEET

For each of the long-term personal, professional, or financial goals you've set for yourself, answer the following questions using as much detail as possible. Remember, you're answering these questions for yourself. Nobody else needs to see your responses, so writing out honest answers will offer you the greatest benefit. As you begin working toward achieving each goal, review the answers you provide in this worksheet often. This action will keep you focused, on schedule, and motivated.

Describe one of your long-term career-related goals: _____

_____

_____

_____

Why have you set this goal? _____

_____

_____

_____

What is the ultimate outcome you plan to achieve? _____

_____

_____

_____

How will achieving this outcome benefit you personally, professionally, and financially in the short- and long-term? _____

_____

_____

_____

What steps do you plan to take in order to achieve this goal? (Summarize your action plan.) _____

_____

_____

_____

What obstacles or challenges do you anticipate encountering? How will you deal with these potential setbacks? _____

_____

_____

_____

In what time frame do you anticipate being able to achieve your long-term goal? (Set a deadline for yourself. If you've divided up your long-term goal into a series of smaller, more readily achievable short-term goals, associate deadlines with each of these smaller objectives in order to keep yourself on track.) _____

_____

_____

_____

Outside of your own skill set, educational background, and work experience, what other resources will you need to tap in order to achieve this goal? (List specific network contacts or other resources you plan to utilize.)

_____

_____

_____

TOOLS TO HELP YOU ACHIEVE SUCCESS

Throughout this book, various tools have been described that you can acquire and use to help you become more organized or that can make achieving your various goals easier. Remember, the goal in using any of these tools is to make your life easier, help you become more organized, assist you in making the most of your valuable time, and to help make your life more clutter-free.

Depending on your own personality, what you do for a living, and your specific needs, some of these tools may not prove to be useful (or some may work much better for you than others). Define what your needs are and how each of the tools you decide to utilize can and will benefit you, then choose to incorporate only those tools into your life that make the most sense in terms of maximizing your time, energy, and financial resources. For example, many people can benefit from using a cellular phone to maximize their down time when they're away from their office or while commuting. For some people, however, simply having a pager will be beneficial, while others can utilize the power of a cell phone that also connects to the Internet (making wireless Web surfing possible).

CHOOSING THE BEST TOOLS TO MEET YOUR NEEDS

Some of the tools described throughout this book include:

- Traditional (Printed) Personal Planners—These planners, from Day-Timer, Franklin Covey, and dozens of other companies, come in a wide range of sizes and formats. These tools are ideal for keeping track of daily, weekly, or monthly schedules, maintaining "To-Do" lists, and storing contact information. This type of tool allows you to stay organized and carefully plan and evaluate how you'll spend your time.
- Scheduling/Contact Management Software—For those who are computer literate and have access to a desktop or laptop computer, scheduling/contact management software (Personal Information Managers) can be used to accomplish the same tasks as a traditional personal planner. All of your scheduling and contact information is more readily available, because you can search your electronic data based on virtually any criteria. These software packages, such as Act! 2000, for example, offer capabilities that simply aren't available using a traditional printed planner.
- Personal Digital Assistants (PDAs)—These powerful handheld devices are the ideal solution for people who need access to notes, contact information, their appointment schedule, and other functionality virtually anywhere they happen to be. These battery-powered devices are becoming increasingly powerful and now offer almost all the capabilities of a personal computer, but in the palm of your hand. To increase the power of these devices, traditional and wireless modems can be connected to units, such as the Palm V,

allowing someone to surf the Web, send and receive e-mail, and gather data off the Internet from anywhere.

- Laptop Computers—When you need all of the power and functionality of a desktop computer while on the go, a laptop computer is the ideal solution. Any PC-based software package that operates on your current PC-based desktop computer will operate flawlessly on a laptop, and data can be exchanged between your desktop and laptop computers with ease (via direct connection cable, a modem connection, Intranet, local-area network (LAN), or an Internet-based connection, for example).

- Desktop Computers—Being able to create, manage, edit, store, and print vast amounts of data is becoming increasingly important, no matter what occupation you're in. Computers now impact virtually every aspect of our lives. While you may have access to a computer at your job, it can also be an advantage to have a computer at home. Having basic computer skills is becoming an absolute must. These are skills that more and more employers are demanding, even if a specific job doesn't require the use of a computer.

- Wireless/Traditional Internet Devices (for Web surfing and e-mail)—Every month, millions of people begin surfing the Web for the first time. In addition to the ability to send and receive e-mail, which has become a common way for people from all walks of life to communicate, an incredible amount of information is available on the Web and accessible to anyone at all times. The power of the Web can be utilized in many ways, by just about everyone, to help move your career forward.

- Cell Phones—In today's business world, people communicate in many different ways. People meet in person, talk on the phone, send and receive faxes, send and receive e-mail, send and receive traditional correspondence using the United States Postal Service, and utilize overnight courier services (such as FedEx, UPS, Airborne, and DHL) when packages and letters need to be received overnight. Never before in history have there been so many ways to communicate. These days, just having a phone at work and at home isn't always enough. People who are on the move, who commute, or who find themselves away from a traditional phone for extended periods of time, find the cell phone to be a powerful tool for staying in touch with coworkers, clients, customers, bosses, friends, vendors, and others—no matter where they are. Digital cellular phone service, from companies like Sprint PCS, AT&T, Cellular One, and countless others, have become increasingly more powerful and cost effective. For those traveling around the world, to places like Europe, GSM-compatible digital cell phones allow for calls to be made from anywhere, often for far less than the cost of using a public pay phone and/or a (prepaid) phone card.

- Pagers—For those who need to receive numeric pages or short text messages, a pager continues to be a lower-cost alternative to a cell phone. Local, regional, and nationwide pager coverage is available. For example, SkyTel (www.skytel.com) offers nationwide one-way text paging for under $25.00 per month.

Before acquiring any of these tools, ask yourself the following questions:

What organizational or productivity tool(s) do you plan to utilize?

_____

_____

How will you utilize each tool?_____

_____

_____

How will the tool help you stay better organized, save time, or save money? _____

_____

_____

How much time will utilizing the tool(s) require? How much time will you save every day, week, or month through the use of the tool?

_____

_____

What is the learning curve required for utilizing the tool? (How will you acquire the skills needed to utilize it?) _____

_____

What is the cost (up-front and ongoing) associated with using the tool? _____

_____

How will implementing one or more of the tools described in this book change your work habits, personal life, or how you manage your finances? _____

_____

THE FINAL CHECKLIST

Every good coach has his or her own playbook and spends countless hours developing strategies and planning for the next game or competition. As your own personal career coach, it's your job to create strategies, plan your own career goals, and define your own career path. If you've read this book from start to finish, you've discovered what needs to be done in order to pursue your goals, interests, and dreams.

Unfortunately, to achieve success, it requires a lot more than just showing up for work and meeting the core responsibilities of your job. Based on what you've already read, the following is a checklist that summarizes the key steps to achieving success. Combine these steps with hard work, dedication, and perseverance, and you'll be well on your way to achieving whatever it is you've set out to accomplish . . . and more!

_____ Develop an understanding of the current personal, professional, and financial situation you're in, and consider what needs to be improved.

_____ Identify your personal and professional strengths and weaknesses.

_____ Begin formulating your long-term personal, professional, and financial goals.

_____ Develop a true understanding of what you want the outcome to be for each goal you pursue.

_____ Understand specifically why you're attempting to achieve each goal. How will you benefit? How will your employer benefit? How will those around you benefit? Why is the outcome of the goal important to you?

_____ Divide each of your long-term goals into smaller, more manageable goals, and then create a timeline and deadlines for achieving those mini-goals.

_____ Identify the obstacles preventing your success. Predicting what obstacles and challenges you'll encounter before they happen will make you better prepared to deal with whatever situations arise.

_____ Develop a true understanding of your personal and professional skill set. What makes you unique? What makes you marketable to potential employers and valuable to your current employer? Determine what knowledge, skills, and experience you still need to acquire.

_____ Decide how and when you'll acquire the additional skills and/or expertise you need or want in order to achieve your long-term goals.

_____ Create a series of action plans for accomplishing each of your goals, objectives, and dreams.

_____ Try to avoid taking on too many responsibilities at once. In a typical day, only try to juggle three or four major issues or tasks. Whenever possible, delegate smaller, less important tasks to others, so that you can focus your time and energy on what's truly important.

_____ Learn how to prioritize the tasks you need to accomplish and focus your energies and attention on the most important tasks when you're the most alert and productive.

_____ Perfect your time management and organizational skills so you can make the most of your time and become as productive as possible. If necessary, begin utilizing an organizational or time management tool, such as a personal planner or PDA, to assist you in becoming and staying organized.

_____ As you define your career path, make sure that each job you pursue will help move your career forward.

_____ Make sure your image, personality, and attitude are all consistent with what you're attempting to achieve. Your outward appearance, your body language, your personality, and how you treat others all contribute to the first impression you make and to what people ultimately will think of you.

_____ One of your long-term and ongoing strategies should be to develop a positive reputation for yourself. Make sure others perceive you to be a hard working, dedicated, honest, friendly, outgoing, and sincere individual who is a team player. Remember, it's difficult to achieve a positive personal and professional reputation, but it only takes one mistake or indiscretion to destroy your good reputation.

_____ When trying to achieve success don't reinvent the process. Pinpoint people whom you admire, who have already achieved the type of success that you're seeking, and determine specifically what they've done to achieve their success. Throughout your career, take advantage of role models and mentors to help you define your career path, make important decisions, and decide the best actions to take.

_____ Never compromise your values or morals when it comes to fitting in or trying to project a specific image.

_____ Create and manage your network and learn how to utilize your network as a powerful resource for accomplishing goals and objectives.

_____ Uncover hidden opportunities and take advantage of them. As you pursue your goals, always be on the lookout for new opportunities. When necessary, create your own opportunities. Don't sit around waiting for opportunities to be dropped in your lap.

_____ Know how and when to take risks. Risk taking should not be something you're afraid to do, especially if you take risks based on the wealth of knowledge and research you've worked hard to acquire before making any important decisions.

_____ Take advantage of whatever tools and resources are available to help you achieve whatever it is you're trying to accomplish.

_____ Throughout your career, especially when you encounter obstacles or problems, never lose sight of your goals and objectives. Keep reminding yourself why you're working to achieve the goals you've set for yourself, and what achieving those goals will mean to you. Also, determine for yourself what motivates you and take positive steps to insure you're able to stay focused and motivated.

_____ Surround yourself with a positive support system that will provide you with an endless supply of support, love and encouragement. Your support system should be made of people whom you care about and respect, and whom you can turn to in times of need for advice and other forms of support—emotional or otherwise.

_____ Maintain a carefully balanced personal, professional, and spiritual life. Make time for the people you care about, but find ways of doing this without neglecting your professional responsibilities. Likewise, avoid neglecting your personal or family obligations, especially when you're needed the most by those you truly care about.

_____ Don't allow the negative attitudes of others to get in your way. If you truly believe you can accomplish something, and you're willing to put forth your very best in order to achieve a specific goal, don't allow anyone to tell you it's not possible or you're not capable of doing it.

_____ Make sure you have a passion for what you're doing. Those who enjoy their work tend to achieve greater levels of success, while experiencing less work-related stress. Pinpoint the aspects of your career you truly enjoy. As you seek out new jobs as you move along your career path, focus on opportunities that will allow you to focus primarily on what you enjoy and what you're good at. Ideally, you want the job you're in to be as close to your ultimate dream job as possible.

Now that you have the core knowledge and know-how to set and achieve your goals, it's time to put forth the energies necessary to begin making your goals and dreams a reality. Remember, as you set out to achieve your goals, always focus on the desired outcome and what it will take to achieve that outcome. Knowing that you'll face pitfalls, obstacles, and challenges, try to pinpoint what you'll encounter in advance and develop contingency plans. This planning will help you to focus your energy better when something unexpected happens, yet keep you firmly on your path toward success.

At this point, you know what you need to do and how you're going to do it. What the future holds for you is entirely up to you!

A P P E N D I X A

case studies

POORVI KUMAR
Advertising Sales Assistant, 3 years
San Francisco, California
25 years old

POORVI HAS BEEN working as an Advertising Sales Assistant at a magazine for three years now. She enjoys the fast pace of the job and the variety of tasks she must complete, but she hasn't had a promotion, title change, or raise in the past year and a half. In addition, Poorvi works from 50 to 70 hours a week, leaving her with little free time to spend with friends and family. She's dong well financially and therefore living comfortably—she makes about $50,000 a year—but she feels like she is definitely qualified to fill a job title higher than the assistant position that she currently fills. Here is some of her experience:

- Bachelor's Degree in Communications, specializing in media relations (heavy emphasis on graphic design)
- Three years experience researching companies, organizations
- Internship in marketing and sales at magazine

- Internship as graphic assistant at publishing company
- Editorial intern at publishing company
- Copyediting and proofreading class

In fact, many of her daily tasks definitely would be tasks for which a manager would be responsible. Her most marketable skill is the diversity of experience she has gained in her various internships and jobs; her skills are diverse and many.

WEAKNESSES

To this point her biggest weakness has been her lack of initiative and willingness to stand up for herself. When she started three years ago in her current position, her supervisors told her that she would have much more creative input on projects. Although she does not have the level of input that she expected based on her offer of employment, she has not ever mentioned her desire to work more creatively doing what she studied in college.

Poorvi decided it was time to evaluate her situation to see what she could do to make her life better. She began by taking some time to think about her goals. What follows is her self-analysis, complete with her goals and priorities.

GOALS

Personal: I think that my goal is a more balanced personal life— spending more time with my friends and doing more "cultural" things, mostly just getting out and about and taking better advantage of all that the Bay Area has to offer. I also want to join an organization from which I can find support from other women in media who have already done things similar to what I want to do. I've mostly let my professional life take over without maintaining any sort of balance and I've let my personal life flounder. Ideally, looking forward, I would like to establish roots here so that I can eventually start my magazine and family here.

Professional: I need to make a job change—probably a lateral move within the magazine so that I can learn more about how the entire magazine creation process works. My long-term goal was always to have my own magazine. And while I don't have the money or skill set to do that just yet, I know that working in another department of a magazine, like editorial or production, would really help keep my goal in motion. I am stuck in this marketing and sales rut—I am doing the same things that I was doing two years ago and therefore, I feel like I have strayed from my main professional goal by focusing too much time and energy on sales and marketing—two parts of the magazine I know are tremendously important, but are not my favorite focus. I have a good background in media relations, graphic design, photography, editing, and even managing layout.

Financial: Obviously, living in the Bay Area is expensive. Luckily I am young and single, without any debt—loans or credit cards. I want to start putting 10 percent of my monthly pay into a 401K, and I am going to start doing research on some investing. I have an old friend from college who works on Wall Street—he should be a good resource. Eventually I am going to need to have some money to start my magazine, so I should start thinking about making some financial contacts and also saving some money to start the magazine. In the long term I want to build a financially sound and stable magazine.

PRIORITIES

1. Change job
2. Join a media group (research online)
3. Make some new friends and contacts while doing something professionally satisfying
4. Gain some new experience in another field

5. Make some extra money and start saving and investing for the magazine and my (eventual) family

Below is Poorvi's broad action plan, which she broke into small, manageable steps.

· ·

ACTION PLAN

Talk to Marcy (my boss) about recommendations to either the production or editorial staff. There is an assistant editor position available right now in editorial that I want to apply for.

Also, talk to Mark in production and Lance in editorial to see if there are any positions available in which I could work. (Don't forget to emphasize strong graphic/media background and copyediting and proofreading class!) I need to make it clear that a new position will not require more work hours per week. Working less than I do now would allow me both to develop my personal life and establish some outside contacts who will, hopefully, be supportive and helpful down the road.

Join a media group—research online.

Ask around for and take some freelance writing jobs to gain some more writing experience and make some more money for financial goals.

· ·

RESULTS

Poorvi spoke with her boss, who definitely understood her concerns. Although she was a little upset that Poorvi wanted to change positions and departments, she understood that Poorvi had taken the original position under the assumption that she would get to learn more about all the parts of the magazine—not just sales and marketing. She decided to take a job in production, where she could get some good experience, and also work closely with editorial to understand how that department works. After she expressed her interest in the editorial process, they offered her the opportunity to write some short pieces for the magazine and website. In addition, she joined a media group based in San Francisco and made some new friends with similar interests—some of her new acquaintances are also very interested in her magazine project.

FUTURE

Once Poorvi decided to take some initiative and take some control of her life, she sprang into action. Although her new job is challenging and different from anything she has ever done before, she is gaining valuable experience that will, eventually, greatly benefit her long-term goal of owning and running her own magazine.

She plans to work in production for at least another year or two, until she feels comfortable with the processes of both editorial and production. Then she plans to begin rounding up some people who are interested in her project so that they can begin drafting preliminary business and action plans to get started on her magazine.

JAMES MARTIN
Help Desk Supervisor
Omaha, Nebraska
29 years old

JAMES HAS BEEN working as help desk supervisor for a large insurance company for four years. He has been promoted several times since he was hired and is a valued employee at his company. He has enjoyed working as a manager for the last two years, and has discovered that he has a talent for motivating people and running a strong department, but he's ready for some new challenges. He's reached the top of the ladder in his department and thinks that he'd like to apply his skills in a new arena. He is doing well financially, and is ready to buy a home. He also wants to get married and start a family, and wants to expand his social life so this will be possible. Finally, his mother, who lives in Sacramento, California, is recently widowed and has some health problems. James wants to make sure that he is able to support her emotionally and financially. Here is a brief history of James's life so far:

- Graduated from UCLA with a degree in history
- Worked on the governor's campaign and then worked as an aide in his press office
- Moved to Omaha to be with a now former girlfriend, and worked as a reporter for the local newspaper
- James decided that reporting wasn't the right career for him and took some courses at a local college so he could pursue his interest in computing
- After completing his courses he was hired as a technician at the insurance company and has enjoyed a successful career there.

STRENGTHS

- Great with people; James is outgoing and friendly
- Strong leadership
- Diverse experience
- Excellent writing skills
- Creative problem solve

WEAKNESSES

- Tends to underestimate his abilities
- Can become overly involved in work to the neglect of his personal life

- Can be reticent about tackling big problems, and tends to shy away from conflict

James knew that he wanted to make some important changes in his life and felt a little overwhelmed. He was having trouble setting priorities and deciding which problem to tackle first. Here is how James followed the advice in *Your Career* to reach his goals.

GOALS

Personal: I want to explore returning to California, since I'm not sure that Omaha is where I want to settle down. I want to become a homeowner within the next year. I want to expand my social life so that I can meet some new people and hopefully someone I might want to get serious about. I want to make sure that my mother is taken care of.

Professional: In the next six months, I want to find a new, challenging work situation. I've reached the top of the ladder in my department and the insurance industry doesn't really interest me. I'd like to find a job that utilizes my writing skills and interest in politics as well as my computer expertise. I'd like a job that is more integral to the functioning of the company, less of a support role. Ultimately, I want to be more of a decision maker. My dream has always been to run for local political office.

Financial: I'm pretty comfortable and I need to stay at my current income level of $60,000, or improve it, in order to achieve my goal of owning my home. I have some investments and have been contributing 8% of my salary to a 401K for the last five years. I want to make sure that I can continue to save for my retirement in whatever job situation I find.

PRIORITIES

1. Conduct research into job and housing market and make a decision about relocating
2. Find a new challenging job
3. Find and purchase a home
4. Develop social life
5. Get more involved with local politics and further develop political connections

Here is James's action plan, which he broke down into smaller manageable steps with deadlines.

ACTION PLAN

November: Research online and through contacts regarding housing and job market in Omaha and San Francisco/Sacramento. Set up informational interviews for when I'm home for Thanksgiving. Look at some properties when I'm home. Make a decision about relocating.

December: Update resume and begin job search. *(James creates two action plans one for California and one for Omaha, since he first needs to make his decision about moving.)*

California: Call my former colleagues from the governor's office for possible leads and to explore my options. Talk to Walter Sherman, Uncle Jack's law partner; his son works for the Democratic committee in Sacramento. Contact headhunters San Francisco and Sacramento. Search online.

Omaha: Call my contacts from Sharon Smith's campaign (note: Bob Perez has a software design company). Call Justin and Mark and let them know I'm looking. Call headhunter. Search online.

Next year: Start housing search. Purchase new home within the year. Join at least one or two local organizations/activities and get involved in local politics.

RESULTS

James's research helped him to decide that he wanted to move back to California. He started his job search in December as planned and decided that he would move to Sacramento in January. James moved before he found the ideal job, but he knew that with his computer expertise he could earn a good living as a temp until he found the right job.

He conducted a thorough job search over the next several months. His uncle's law partner's son, Dan Sherman, put him in touch with a friend who ran a political consulting firm in Sacramento who was looking for someone with strong technical skills to design and manage the company's database and website. James interviewed and felt the job offered him the opportunity to combine his interest in politics and his computer expertise. He doesn't do much writing for his job, but he decided that on the whole this job was a really strong match with his goals. He is part of the management team and is involved in all the decisions made by the company.

The company is fairly small and has a very social atmosphere so his personal life has already picked up. However, the job is very demanding and James had to make sure that he stuck to his action plan and made the time to meet his personal goals. In March, James noticed that he was working late every night and even on the weekends. He went back to his plan and noticed that he had neglected to follow through on his goal to join some local organizations.

He started volunteering for a youth sports league, and has made some great friends as well as contacts in the community. His job has involved him in politics as he wished, and he has started to explore the possibility of running for city council. Through these activities and through some people he got back in touch with in the course of his job search, James has started to meet some women to date.

James found that he had to readjust his plan for purchasing a home. The move to California was more expensive than he planned for so he had to dip into his savings. James decided to save some more money this year so that he can have more flexibility when looking for a house next year. He likes his apartment and is still getting reacquainted with the city so he doesn't think of this as a major setback.

James also sees his mother fairly regularly and was reminded that his mother is very well connected in the community. She has volunteered for local committees all her life and seems to know just about everyone in town. James's mom has proved to be great resource, and he has learned a lot about local politics.

FUTURE

James feels that he is on track to meet his goals. His job is just what he hoped and he's building ties in the community. He is enjoying having a more active social life. He has set his goal of owning a home back by one year, but knows that he is taking the right steps to make this happen.

He plans to run for city council in two years. And he has started dating the woman who runs the youth sports league, and he hopes that the relationship continues to progress.

resources

BOOKS

50 Ways to Get Promoted. Nathan G. Jensen, Rick Wooden. PSI Research-Oasis Press, 1999.

1001 Ways to Get Promoted. David E. Rye. Career Press, 2000.

Be Your Own Executive Coach. Peter Delisser. Chandler House Press, 1999.

Beyond Performance: What Employees Really Need to Know to Climb the Success Ladder. Richard D. Nolen. New Perspectives, 1999.

Career Busters: 22 Things People Do to Mess Up Their Careers and How to Avoid Them. Arthur D. Rosenburg. McGraw-Hill, 1996.

Coach Yourself to Success: 101 Tips for Reaching Your Goals at Work and in Life. Talane Miedaner, Sandy Vilas. Contemporary Books, 2000.

Get Ahead, Stay Ahead!: Learn the 70 Most Important Career Skills, Traits, and Attitudes to: Stay Employed! Get Promoted! Get a Better Job!. Dianna Booher. McGraw-Hill, 1997.

Getting Promoted: Real Strategies for Advancing Your Career. Harry E. Chambers. Perseus Press, 1999.

Going to the Top: A Road Map for Success from America's Leading Woman Executives. Carol A. Gallagher, Susan K. Golant. Viking Press, 2000.

Headhunters Confidential! 125 Insider Secrets to Landing Your Dream Job. Alan R. Schonberg, Robert Shook. McGraw-Hill Professional Publishing, 2000.

High Impact Tools and Activities for Strategic Planning: Creative Techniques for Facilitating Your Organization's Planning Process. Rod Napier, Patrick Sanaghan, Clint Sidle. McGraw-Hill, 1998.

How to Become CEO: The Rules for Rising to the Top of Any Organization. Jeffery J. Fox. Hyperion Press, 1998.

Interview and Salary Negotiation: For Job Hunters, Career Changers, Consultants, and Freelancers. Kate Wendleton. Career Press, 1999.

The Pathfinder: How to Choose or Change Your Career for a Lifetime of Satisfaction and Success. Nicholas Lore. Fireside, 1998.

Secrets of a CEO Coach: Your Personal Training Guide to Thinking Like a Leader and Acting Like a Leader and Acting Like a CEO. D.A. Benton. McGraw-Hill, 1999.

Take Yourself to the Top: The Secrets of America's #1 Career Coach [UNABRIDGED]. Laura Berman Fortgang. Dove Booksellers, 1999.

The Portable Coach: 28 Surefire Strategies for Business and Personal Success. Thomas J. Leonard, Byron Laursen. Scribner, 1998.

Thinking for a Living: Creating New Ideas That Revitalize Your Business, Career, & Life. Joey Rieman. Longstreet Press, 1998.

What Color Is Your Parachute? 2000. Richard Nelson Bolles. Ten Speed Press, 2000.

What Color Is Your Parachute? 2001: A Practical Manual for Job-Hunters and Career-Changers. Richard Nelson Bolles. Ten Speed Press, 2000.

What Color Is Your Parachute Workbook: How to Create a Picture of Your Ideal Job or Next Career. Richard Nelson Bolles. Ten Speed Press, 1998.

ONLINE

Career.com: www.career.com
  Read about featured employers and post your resume online.
CareerBuilder.com: www.careerbuilder.com
  Search for jobs, and career information.
Careerbuzz.com: www.careerbuzz.com
Learn about career opportunities, gather career information, and
  receive career advice.
CareerCity: www.careercity.com/content/careermanage
  Post your resume and plan your career.
CareerMag.com: www.careermag.com
  Search for jobs, post your resume, participate in the message
  board, and read articles.
CareerMosaic & headhunter.net: www.careermosaic.com
  Search for the job of your choice by community or industry,
  gather information from the extensive resource center, and read
  success stories.
CareerShop.com: www.careershop.com
  Post your resume, search for jobs, explore training courses, or
  join the online community of your choice.
Monster.com Career Center:
  content.monster.com/experts/career/library
  Search for jobs, post your resume, gather career advice from the
  career coach library.
The International Coach Federation: www.coachfederation.org
  The official website of a non-profit, professional organization of
  personal and business coaches.
iVillage.com—Work Information:
  www.ivillage.com/hottopics/work/main.html
  A site aimed mostly towards women. Learn how to find a job
  and succeed at work, search for jobs, and read advice from and
  the success stories of other women.

WetFeet.com: www.wetfeet.com

Research companies, get advice from experts, and find a job online.

❶ N D E X